D. L. Moody
on
Spiritual Leadership

D. L. MOODY
on Spiritual Leadership

Steve Miller

MOODY PUBLISHERS
CHICAGO

Library of Congress Cataloging-in-Publication Data

Miller, Steve, 1960–
    D. L. Moody on Spiritual Leadership / by Steve Miller.
    p.cm.
        ISBN 0-8024-1063-4
        1. Moody, Dwight Lyman, 1837–1899. 2. Christian leadership.
        3. Spiritual life. I. Title
BV3785.M7M55 2004
269'.2'092—dc22   2003022653

1 3 5 7 9 10 8 6 4 2

Printed in the United States of America

To every leader and future leader—

May you be encouraged and inspired

as you discover the mighty ways

in which God used D. L. Moody . . .

and the mighty ways He can use you.

CONTENTS

∞

I express my appreciation to the team at Moody Publishers for all their enthusiastic help with this book, particularly Greg Thornton and Mark Tobey as they shared the vision for the book, Jim Vincent for his thoughtful editorial input, and Amy Peterson for her fine author relations work.

And I offer special thanks to two knowledgeable and informative librarians at the Crowell Library at Moody Bible Institute, Wally Osborne and Joe Cataio. Wally graciously welcomed me to make use of the library's fine collection of resources, and Joe provided valuable guidance that saved many hours of research as I worked my way through the library's historical archives.

My deepest gratitude of all goes to my wife, Becky, my three sons, Keith, Nathan, and Ryan, and my mother, Betty Miller, for showing constant support to me and enthusiasm for this project all through the many late nights and weekends I worked on it.

The Leader God Uses

This is not your typical book on spiritual leadership. That's because Dwight Lyman Moody was not your typical spiritual leader.

There were many reasons Moody should never have become one of the most prominent evangelists and ministers of his day. He had none of the credentials expected of spiritual leaders. He had no formal ministry training. He didn't take the tried-and-true paths to leadership that other Christian leaders had taken. And when he began serving God, he could barely read and write.

Put another way, he had significant limitations . . . many of them.

But Moody knew he worked for a God who has no limitations. Early in his ministry, he learned a powerful truth that shaped everything he did. He came to realize God can use any Christian to accomplish His work. And when Christians surrender themselves unreservedly to Him, He's free to work unreservedly through them.

In other words, our great God can do very extraordinary works through very ordinary people.

Moody believed that all Christians have a place of service to the Lord—not just leaders. He relied heavily on the help of "average" Christians in his evangelistic meetings everywhere. He saw the masses of believers in the pews as a tremendous source of untapped power—as armies who could help advance Christ's kingdom even if ministry never became their occupation. He started schools to equip these businesspeople, laborers, homemakers, students, and others, giving them practical training they could use to serve God in the course of their everyday lives. This way of thinking made Moody an unconventional and even revolutionary figure in nineteenth-century Christendom.

His contemporaries couldn't argue with the results. Everywhere Moody spoke, he and his staff trained up multitudes of helpers to meet one-on-one with those who, through Moody's messages, wanted to receive Christ. And out of the huge crowds who heard Moody speak, many became believers. Real and lasting change took place in most of these lives—these weren't just flash-in-the-pan conversions. Large numbers of people were added to local churches whenever Moody visited a city or region. And it was all possible because Moody believed laypeople could be equipped to help make ministry happen.

In time, many of the greatest spiritual leaders of that era came to respect Moody and strongly supported his endeavors. He spoke in some of their churches, and they spoke at his world-renowned training conferences and schools. Moody did not consider himself one of them because he was well aware of what he lacked in comparison to them. He looked up to them and, with abounding enthusiasm, learned from them at every opportunity he could. And yet they embraced him as a fellow spiritual leader because it was clear he was being used powerfully by God to change many, many lives.

What exactly was it that made Moody so effective as a spiritual leader? He had the inner qualities that are absolutely essential in every Christian leader's life. He might not have had the diploma on the wall or the knowledge to debate the finer points of theology, but he possessed the right heart and the right attitudes, and that made him wholly moldable clay in the hands of the Master Potter.

D. L. Moody's example is powerful proof for us that it's the right kind of person God uses—not the right program, right methods, or right techniques. Effective spiritual leadership is all about the person; it is not a five-step process, a ten-part formula, nor some other set of supposedly guaranteed guidelines. While it's always beneficial to develop our leadership skills and to grow in our biblical knowledge, ultimately, these tools are worthless if we're not the kind of vessels God can use.

In this book we will discover the inner qualities that made D. L. Moody a leader God could use in mighty ways—qualities that are important for any spiritual leader to emulate. We'll learn what needs to happen in our inner lives so that we're more effective in our outer lives. For as Moody has shown, it's not having all the right credentials that makes us the kind of leaders God can use. It's being the right person.

Is that your heart's desire?

ᴬLife
Fully Surrendered
ᵗᵒ God

> "For the eyes of the Lord run to and fro throughout the whole earth, to show Himself strong on behalf of those whose heart is loyal to Him."
>
> —2 Chronicles 16:9

When Dwight Lyman Moody set out to see the world at the tender age of seventeen, God and Christianity were far from his mind. He was determined to make himself rich—and to leave behind the backbreaking farm labor and poverty that had defined his youth.

Because Moody's father had died unexpectedly when Dwight and his siblings were young, his mother struggled hard to feed and care for the family, with the children working and contributing whatever sustenance they could as they grew older. Though Moody was respectful of his mother and loved her, he was also restless and wanted to break away from the monotony of life in rural New England. Eager for material success, he left home and headed for Boston—with several strikes against him. He had no money, no place to stay, and no assurance of a job, and he was barely literate, with only about four or five patchwork years of schooling.

Through the years, Dwight's mother, Betsy, had read to the children from a Bible at night. Evidently the seeds had not taken root in Dwight's heart, for he showed no interest in spiritual matters at the time he left home. For several days he walked the streets of Boston in search of a job, but without success. His earthy country-boy attire and rough mannerisms evoked stares of contempt and ridicule from the city-cultured Bostonians and raised doubts in the minds of prospective employers. Dwight's uncle, Samuel Holton, had a shoe store in town, but initially Dwight was too prideful to ask his relative for a job; he also knew his uncle to be a stern taskmaster. Besides, this same uncle had earlier told him to stay away from Boston because he wouldn't fit in well.

After several days of fruitless searching, Moody humbled himself and asked his uncle Samuel for work. Samuel was willing to hire the young man—but with two stipulations: First, the hardheaded youth had to be willing to adhere to his uncle's exacting methods of work, and second, he was to attend church with his uncle each Sunday.

Moody's attendance at church was regular, but his chief pre-occupation continued to be financial gain. Then one day Moody's Sunday school teacher, Edward Kimball, came to the shoe store to talk with Moody. Kimball's visit led the young man to a spiritual awakening:

When I was in Boston I used to attend a Sunday school class, and one day I recollect my teacher came around behind the counter of the shop I was at work in, and put his hand upon my shoulder, and talked to me about Christ and my soul. I had not felt that I had a soul till then. I said to myself: "This is a very strange thing. Here is a man who never saw me till lately, and he is weeping over my sins, and I never shed a tear about them." . . . It was not long after that I was brought into the Kingdom of God.[1]

∞

–MOODY'S FIRST GOAL: $100,000–

After Moody became a Christian, he continued to attend church and work for his uncle. But eventually youthful rest-lessness beckoned again for him to move onward, and in the fall of 1856 he took a train westward to Chicago, a wild and fast-growing city that abounded with opportunities for aggressive young men like Moody. Chicago was also a much better fit with his personality, as he had always felt out of place in the high-society populace in Boston and at his uncle's church. By this time, Moody had set his sights on building a personal fortune of $100,000.

It didn't take long for Moody to find work in the Windy City. Taking advantage of the experience gleaned from his uncle's business, he was hired at a footwear store. His drive for personal gain must have been obvious, as one of the proprietors said of him, "His ambition made him anxious to lay up money."[2] And one of Moody's fellow clerks observed,

> Moody was a first-rate salesman. It was his particular pride to make his column foot up the largest of any on the book, not only in the way of sales, but also of profits. He took particular delight in trading with notional or unreasonable people; especially when they made great show of smartness and cunning, and thought themselves extraordinarily wise. Nothing was ever misrepresented in the smallest particular; but when it came to be a question of sharpness and wit between buyer and seller, Moody generally had the best of it.[3]

It was evident by now that when Moody devoted his energies to a task, he didn't do so halfheartedly. He went all out, holding nothing back. And no one else could keep up with him.

Within four years, Moody had saved up around $10,000—no small feat in a day when most men seldom earned more than a few hundred dollars per year. He was making solid progress toward his financial goal. But during this time, another passion began to burn within him. Upon arriving in Chicago, he had dutifully become a regular churchgoer, but a notable turn took place in his heart during his first year in the Windy City. A spiritual awakening of sorts swept the city, and in a letter written to his mother on January 6, 1857, Moody wrote, "There is a great revival of religion in this city."[4] Up to this time Moody had been actively inviting people off the streets to attend church with him, yet he hadn't taken steps to show personal concern for their spiritual condition. But during this period of revival, Moody met and came under the care of Christian mentors who inspired him to take a more serious interest in prayer, spiritual growth, and evangelism.

–PUTTING GOD'S WILL FIRST–

Moody's zeal in spiritual endeavors grew quickly and soon matched the diligence he applied to his business dealings. In time, Moody's passion for ministering to people—particularly the poorest children in Chicago—grew to the point where it was a challenge for him to divide his energies between church and business. While Moody still lacked in personal spiritual development and ministry skills, he experienced tremendous success in his church work. As a result, the varied demands upon his time grew greater. What's more, he sensed God's calling upon his life—a calling for him not just to serve the Lord but to make it his full-time occupation. Some twenty-five years later at a Christian workers' conference, Moody related the struggle in this way:

∞

When I came to Jesus Christ, I had a terrible battle to surrender my will, and to take God's will. When I gave up business, I had another battle for three months, and I fought against it. It was a terrible battle. But oh! how many times I have thanked God that I gave up my will and took God's will.[5]

∞

In 1861 Moody made the decision to step out in faith and leave the business world. All through the first half of the 1860s, he was actively involved in numerous avenues of ministry, including the YMCA and speaking to Union soldiers in Civil War camps. In 1867, again Moody struggled when he felt God calling him—this time, the call was to take his ministry beyond the city of Chicago.

∞

Then there was another time when God was calling me into higher service, to go out and preach the gospel all over the land, instead of staying in Chicago. I

> *fought against it for months; but the best thing I ever did was when I surrendered my will, and let the will of God be done in me.*
>
> *If you take my advice, you will have no will other than God's will. Make a full and complete surrender.*[6]

∞

It was from this time onward that Moody's ministry would never be the same, experiencing continuous explosive growth in the decades to come.

Pursuing Heavenly Treasures . . .

The key to Moody's tremendous business success was his all-consuming drive to be the very best at what he did. And though in his early years of ministry he had much to learn, there's one truth he recognized immediately: Any work done for the Lord ought to be carried out to the very best of our ability. As Moody said, "When [God] gave Christ to this world, He gave the best He had, and He wants us to do the same."[7]

Thus Moody went from pouring every ounce of his energy into building up treasures here on earth to building up treasures in heaven. Just as he had held nothing back in his ambitious pursuits in the business world, he now held nothing back in his spiritual endeavors. To him, doing anything less was unthinkable.

. . . And Total Surrender to God

Moody's conviction that Christians ought to live in total surrender to God was reinforced in the early years of his ministry while in England. There he heard British evangelist Henry Varley say, "The world has yet to see what God will do with and for and through and in and by the man who is fully and wholly consecrated to Him."[8] Moody thought to himself,

∞

He said "a man." He did not say a great man, nor a learned man, nor a rich man, nor a wise man, nor an eloquent man, nor a smart man, but simply "a man." I am a man, and it lies with the man himself whether he will or will not make that entire and full consecration. I will try my uttermost to be that man.[9]

∞

Henry Varley's encouragement had a tremendous impact on Moody, who, because of his lack of education and ministry training, faced frequent reminders that, from a human perspective, in many ways he was inadequate. Yet as he came to realize that it is God who does the actual work of ministry and that the most effective channel for ministry is a wholly surrendered life, he resolved more than ever to avail himself completely for the Lord's use.

All through his years of ministry, Moody shared these discoveries with his fellow believers and constantly urged them to fully yield their lives to God.

∞

One of the sweetest lessons we can learn in the school of Christ is the surrender of our wills to God, letting Him plan for us and rule our lives. . . . I cannot look a day into the future. I do not know what is going to happen tomorrow; in fact, I do not know what may happen before night; so that I cannot choose for myself as well as God can choose for me; and it is much better to surrender my will to God's will.[10]

The first thing a man must do if he desires to be used in the Lord's work, is to make an unconditional surrender of himself to God. He must consecrate *and then* concentrate. *A man who does not put his whole life into one channel does not count for much, and the man who only goes into work with half a heart does not amount to much* [emphasis added].[11]

It seems about the hardest thing, to get to the end of self, but when we have got to the end of self, and self is lost sight of, self-seeking and self-glory thrown aside, and Christ and His cause are uppermost in our hearts, how easy it is for God to use us.[12]

∞

Not only did Moody urge that Christians make themselves fully available, but he warned of the potential danger of half-hearted service. To illustrate his point, he would speak of when God called Abraham to leave Ur of the Chaldees and go to Canaan:

Then [Abram] came to Haran, which is about halfway . . . and stayed there—we do not know just how long, but probably about five years.

Now, I believe that there are a great many Christians who are what might be called Haran Christians. They go to Haran, and there they stay. They only half obey. They are not out-and-out. How was it that God got him out of Haran? His father died. The first call was to leave Ur of the Chaldees and go into Canaan, but instead of going all the way they stopped half-way, and it was affliction that drove Abram out of Haran. A great many of us bring afflictions on ourselves, because we are not out-and-out for the Lord. We do not obey Him fully. God had plans He wanted to work out through Abram, and He could not work them out as long as he was there in Haran. Affliction came, and then we find that he left Haran, and started for the Promised Land.[13]

—GIVING GOD THE CREDIT—

It's when we're totally surrendered that God has the freedom to accomplish the work He desires to do through us. And it's vital we always remember that it's God Himself who is doing that work. It is He who brings forth the results, not us:

∞

It wasn't David or the sling, but it was the God of David. It wasn't Samson, but the God of Samson. It wasn't Joshua, but the God of Joshua. It wasn't the rod of Moses that did the work, but it was the God of Moses. And, my dear friends, what we want is to learn that lesson.[14]

If we are lifted up and say we have got such great meetings and such crowds are coming, and get to thinking about crowds and about the people, and get our minds off from God, and are not constantly in communion with Him, lifting our hearts in prayer, this work will be a stupendous failure.[15]

You have got nothing to be proud of. If you are ever used at all, bear in mind that it is God speaking in you, and not you yourself.

We do not say that gas pipe gives the light; it only conveys it. If we have any light in us, it is Christ's

*light. Let us be careful that we do not fall into that
sin of being proud and lifted up.*[16]

*We want the great, the mighty, but God takes the
foolish things, the despised things, the things which are
not. What for? That no flesh may glory in His sight.*[17]

–WHAT DOES GOD EXPECT OF US?–

Now, in all this talk about total surrender, inevitably a question
arises: Does such a commitment mean going into full-time
Christian ministry, as D. L. Moody did?

Absolutely not, Moody would say. In fact, Moody constantly
lamented the fact that so few Christians realized how much
God could use them right where they were. Yielding ourselves
totally to God doesn't mean becoming a full-time minister or
missionary, but rather, giving our whole heart and the best of
our abilities to whatever opportunities we have for serving
Him. Ministry need not be an office; it's a lifestyle devoted to
attracting the lost to Christ and encouraging other believers in
the faith.

*Every Christian ought to be a worker. He need not
be a preacher, he need not be an evangelist, to be
useful. He may be useful in business. See what*

power [a Christian] employer has, if he likes! How he could labor with his employees in his business relations! Often a man can be far more useful in a business sphere than he could in another.[18]

A false impression has got hold of many of God's people. They have got the idea that only a few can talk about God's affairs. Nine-tenths of people say, if anything is to be done for the souls of men, "Oh, the ministers must do it." It doesn't enter into the hearts of the people that they have any part in the matter. . . . Any one can do this work.[19]

According to Moody, every single believer has a place in the Lord's service. Every person has his or her unique niche, his or her special role. It was this conviction that led Moody to encourage all Christians—even children—toward serving in whatever capacity they could.

If this world is going to be reached, I am convinced it must be done by men and women of average talent. After all there are comparatively few people in the world who have great talents. Here is a man with one talent; there is another with three; perhaps I may have only half a talent. But if we all go to work and

27

trade with the gifts we have the Lord will prosper us; and we may double or treble our talents.[20]

I have little sympathy with the idea that a Christian man or woman has to live for years before they can have the privilege of leading anyone out of the darkness of this world into the kingdom of God. I do not believe, either, that all God's work is going to be done by ministers, and other officers in the Churches. This lost world will never be reached and brought back to loyalty to God, until the children of God wake up to the fact that they have a mission in the world. If we are true Christians we should all be missionaries.[21]

God has a niche for every one of his children. Happy the man or woman who has found his or her place.[22]

Biographer John McDowell noted,

> More than any other man of our times, Dwight L. Moody vindicated the rights, duties and privileges of the layman in carrying the Gospel to the world, as opposed to the exclusive prerogatives of an ordained clergy. . . . Mr. Moody believed that every Christian was foreordained to service; by his own example and his untiring effort he did all he could to help Christians realize their divine call.[23]

28

–NOTHING DONE FOR GOD IS TOO SMALL–

One unfortunate misperception common among lay Christians is that because they're not ministers or leaders, their service is not as significant in advancing God's kingdom. In fact, they may even find themselves reluctant to fulfill the more routine opportunities for service simply because they seem so . . . well, *unimportant*. Yet according to Moody, no work of ministry is a small thing in the eyes of God:

∞

Now, if every one of us did something every day, if it is what we call a little thing, but if it is done for the Master, mark you, it is not a little thing.[24]

Let us go to work and keep at it. Find something to do. Remember that anything you do for God should not be looked upon as an insignificant work.[25]

If each one of us is doing some little thing, it isn't little in the Master's sight. If we keep at it 365 days in the year, there will be a good deal of work done at the end of the year.[26]

There are a great many different ways of doing good. A lady once visited a hospital, and noticed with what pleasure the patients would smell and look at the flowers sent to them. Said she: "If I had known that a bunch of flowers would do so much good, I would have sent some from home."

As soon as she got home, she sent some flowers out of her garden. It was a little thing—a bouquet of flowers. It might be a very insignificant work—very small; but if it was done in the right spirit, God accepted it. A cup of water given in His name is accepted as given to Himself. Nothing that is done for God is small.[27]

∽

Moody also said it's when we're willing to do the little things that God entrusts us with bigger opportunities:

∽

The men who have been permitted to do higher things are the men that began with small things. If you are not willing to deal with one man about his soul, and labor with that one man, you are not fit to go into the pulpit and preach to others. Some of Christ's greatest discourses were given to one person or two persons.[28]

The more we use the means and opportunities we have, the more will our ability and our opportunities be increased.[29]

∽

—GOD WILL MULTIPLY THE FRUIT—

All the way to the end of his life, Moody repeatedly exhorted Christians to *consecrate* themselves and to *concentrate* in their service to the Lord. Consecrate and concentrate—that is, total surrender and total focus. He called for total devotion to the task at hand, no matter how small it was. He knew that if we are faithful to consecrate and concentrate, then the Lord will take care of bringing forth the fruit of ministry. He will take that which is small and multiply its impact—a truth confirmed by this letter from Finland, which was sent to one of Moody's sons shortly after the evangelist's death:

> Are you aware that your father was the means of starting evangelical Christianity in Finland? From an autobiography of Rev. Eric Jansson, "the apostle to Finland," I see that he (Jansson) and his wife were converted under your father's preaching in Chicago and were for a while active members of your father's church, and that the Spirit used a remark made by your father to impress upon Mr. Jansson the duty of going home to his own kindred and his own country and tell what great things the Lord had done for him. Accordingly he returned and has by God's grace made such a record as few have made since the days of the apostles; has endured all kinds of persecution for "the offense of the cross," and has accomplished great things for God. . . . There are now 31 Baptist churches with 2,030 members, in Finland.

244 were baptized last year. Two Baptist papers are published, and the beginning of a theological seminary was made some years ago. I consider Jansson one of your father's greatest trophies, and I regret that I did not write to you about him before. I doubt whether your father himself ever knew how the Lord had used him in Finland, where he has never been.[30]

–THE POSSIBILITIES ARE INFINITE–

Moody never set out to be great in ministry. Rather, he chose simply to be faithful. He yielded himself completely to God, allowing the Lord to use him however He chose. We, too, can make that choice—and allow God to work mightily through us. As Wilbur Chapman noted, "The thing that made Mr. Moody great as a Christian is within the reach of every follower of Christ."[31]

Indeed, the possibilities for service are infinite, according to William Earl Dodge: "The great lesson in Mr. Moody's life is the infinite and magnificent possibility for service which can come to one that puts himself absolutely in God's hand to be used.[32]

MOODY
from the Pulpit

A LITTLE GIRL, only eleven years old, once came to me in a Sunday school and said: "Won't you please pray that God will make me a winner of souls?" . . . Oh, suppose she lives three-score years and goes on winning four or five souls every year; at the end of her journey there will be three hundred souls on the way to glory. And how long will it be before that little company swells to a great army? Don't you see how that little mountain rill keeps swelling till it carries everything before it? Little trickling streams have run into it, till now, a mighty river, it has great cities on its banks, and the commerce of all nations floating on its waters. So when a single soul is won to Christ you cannot see the result. A single one multiplies to a thousand, and that into ten thousand. Perhaps a million shall be the fruit; we cannot tell.[33]

CHAPTER TWO

An Abounding
Love for People

LET ALL THAT YOU DO BE
DONE WITH LOVE.

—1 CORINTHIANS 16:14

That D. L. Moody had by far the largest Sunday school program in all Chicago—bursting at the seams with more than a thousand children—was an amazing feat.

Even more amazing, he founded the program in a notorious part of Chicago nicknamed "Little Hell," using an emptied-out saloon that was surrounded by some two hundred bars and gambling dens.

This district of northern Chicago, commonly known as "the Sands," was a cesspool of sorts, inhabited by the most hardened and dangerous elements of society. At night, crime was rampant and went unchecked. The children who lived in this ramshackle neighborhood were the poorest of the poor, with parents or guardians who were alcoholics or drug abusers. The vast majority of these children were neglected and ill-mannered, and seldom went to school.

So how did Moody manage to attract such large numbers of these children Sunday after Sunday to learn from the Bible and sing Christian songs? The same way he attracted both individuals and multitudes all through his forty-plus years of ministry—with a genuine and compassionate love for them.

When Moody began recruiting children for Sunday school programs at various churches around Chicago, he was distressed that problem children like those from the Sands would show up once and never come back. The needs of these children were vastly different and simply weren't being met. Nor were they accustomed to sitting still, behaving quietly, and studying printed lessons with others who had come from better social and economic backgrounds.

−ACTS OF LOVE FOR CHILDREN
OF "THE SANDS"−

Moody's heart went out to these little misfits of society, and that's when he came up with the idea of renting an empty saloon in the Sands and setting up his own Sunday school program. He thought up many innovative ideas for drawing the children, such as offering them pony rides as he rode through the streets or giving them oranges, peanuts, and candy from his pockets.

Once the children came, he gave them something more important that they all longed for and in most cases weren't getting anywhere else: love. When they saw he really cared about them and wanted to help them, they were won over. Son William Moody said that once children became a part of the program, his father "looked after them, visiting their homes if absent, and taking such a warm and practical interest in them that they became devotedly attached to him."[1]

An 1867 issue of *The Advance,* a Christian magazine, said this about Moody's ways with the children:

> He goes to the door when the bell rings so as to take each child by the hand. He has a word for this one, an admonition for that, and something for all. Much of his success is due to the personality of his efforts. It seems that if all Christians were as earnest and devoted, not only a "State," but the world might be "taken and held for Christ."[2]

Elsewhere we read that he devoted his spare time—and money—on behalf of the neglected children of the Sands. "Time and strength and money he spent freely on their behalf. One of his employers testified that he had known him to supply as many as twenty barefoot urchins with shoes in a single day at his own expense."[3]

If Moody discovered that a child's parents were in great need or sick, he would prepare a basket of fruit, coal, blankets, and other such necessities to drop off at the family's dwelling place.

Moody himself pointed out love as the essential element to winning a responsive audience:

∽

If a Sabbath school teacher does not love his scholars—if he goes to them as if it was a lesson he wished to get over, it will not be long before they find it out. They will see it in his eyes, in his face, in his actions. And so, let us see . . . the necessity of having the love of God in our hearts. . . . If you go . . . from a sense of duty you will make no progress with [them], but if you go to [them] and talk of the love of Christ, and show kindness in your actions, [they] will hear you.[4]

∽

So it was Moody's love for people that drew them in. They welcomed him because he had genuine care for them. His love was real and spoke volumes to them.

–Winning People by Kindness–

Abounding love was one of Moody's dominant traits as a spiritual leader. Fellow preacher and dear friend Henry Drummond said of Moody that "none can stand beside him" in terms of his "sheer goodness and love."[5] W. R. Dale, a minister in England, said Moody "could never speak of a lost soul without tears in his eyes."[6] Biographer John McDowell said Moody "won men by his kindness."[7]

Dr. Charles Goss noted,

> Tears start to the eyes of those who knew Mr. Moody well, at the thought of the absolutely inexhaustible depths of his love for all living things. Horses, dogs, cows, animals, and birds—all excited emotions of his heart. In the realm of human life, love for all classes was a master passion.[8]

And biographer Gamaliel Bradford put it well when he said Moody "carried men with him because he preached to the heart and from the heart."[9]

–The Absolute Necessity of Love–

We can have the most extraordinary ministry abilities and make the greatest sacrifices ever witnessed by the world, but if we don't have love, our efforts are futile, and we are nothing. That was the apostle Paul's point exactly when he said:

Though I speak with the tongues of men and of angels, but have not love, I have become sounding brass or a clanging cymbal. And though I have the gift of prophecy, and understand all mysteries and all knowledge, and though I have all faith, so that I could remove mountains, but have not love, I am nothing. And though I bestow all my goods to feed the poor, and though I give my body to be burned, but have not love, it profits me nothing." (1 Corinthians 13:1–3)

Here's another way to put it: Love can go far in making up for any deficiencies we might have in our service. Love gives us a power that can compensate for the fact that we're not the best speaker or the most skilled worker. In fact, that was Moody's experience. Though at first when he read the Bible to children he had to skip over many words he couldn't read, he had their rapt attention. That's because they knew Moody cared. Moody was fond of saying, "A worker must win the hearts and affections of the people before he can do any effective work."[10]

That's not to say we can allow ourselves to become complacent about possessing less-than-proficient ministry skills. As we grow more capable, we'll find greater usefulness in the Lord's hands. We should always desire to equip ourselves in the best possible way. But if there's one place we cannot be deficient, it's love. Moody believed that and preached it throughout four decades of ministry:

∞

The reason so many preachers have failed is because love has not been the motive power.[11]

A man, though he is deep in learning and theology, if he has not love in his heart he will do no good.[12]

A man may be a good doctor without loving his patients; a good lawyer without loving his clients; a good geologist without loving science; but he cannot be a good Christian without love.[13]

Let us ask ourselves the question: Is love the motive power that urges us to go out and work for God?" . . . Without it a great deal of work will go for naught. The work will be swept away like chaff without it. Christ looks down and examines our hearts and actions, and although our deeds may be great in the eyes of the world, they may not be in His eyes.[14]

∞

–SHOWING SYMPATHY–

A key element of the love we're to show is sympathy. If we want to strike a responsive chord in the hearts of our listeners, we need to place ourselves in their shoes.

∞

The world wants sympathy about as much as any-thing. There are so many we could reach if we could sympathize with them. If we stand upon a higher plane, we won't succeed. The Son of God passed by the mansions and went down in a manger that He might sympathize with the lowly. If we want to reach people, we have got to put ourselves in the places of those people, if we are going to succeed.[15]

I believe there are very few men who cannot be reached if we can only lay our lives beside them and let them know that we sympathize with them. . . . We must lay our lives alongside of the drunkards and gamblers; we have to tell the lost of a better life and a better way in this dark world, and, when they see that we really sympathize with their fallen con-dition, we are going to reach them.[16]

If you want to get into sympathy, put yourself in a man's place. . . . If we haven't got it, pray that we might have it, so that we may be able to reach those men and women that need kindly words and kindly actions far more than sermons. The mistake is that we have been preaching too much and sympathizing too little.[17]

∞

Son William Moody recalled one morning when his father put himself in another man's place:

> One day in later years, when Moody had settled himself for a morning's uninterrupted work, he chanced to look out of the window and saw a student evidently leaving the Conferences for the station and trudging along with an immensely heavy bag. Moody put the matter out of his head, but somehow when he tried to fix his thoughts upon the Bible, always that boy with the heavy bag kept getting in the way. Finally, he says, "I couldn't stand it any longer. I went to the barn and hurriedly had my horse hitched up, overtook the young man, and carried him and his baggage to the station. When I returned to the house I had no further difficulty in fixing my attention on the subject."[18]

–The Power of Love–

Jesus said that all the Law and the Prophets are summed up in just two commandments: Love God, and love your neighbor (Matthew 22:36–40). Ultimately, everything in life comes down to our relationship with God and our relationships with people. And in both, we're to display love. When love is in place, all God's commandments are taken care of. That's because when we possess love—true, biblical love—we won't want to do wrong against the Lord or people.

What's more, Jesus went so far as to say we're to love our enemies (Matthew 5:44). We're to show our love not only to those who love us in return, but to those who hate us. That's exactly what God did, isn't it? "In this is love, not that *we* loved God, but that *He* loved us and sent His Son" (1 John 4:10, italics added). God stepped out and took the initiative to love us even though, before our salvation, we had no love for Him. That's the kind of love He showed, and it's the kind of love we're called to show as well.

When the apostle Paul gave God's own definition of love in 1 Corinthians 13, he made this remarkable statement: "Love never fails. . . . And now abide faith, hope, love, these three; but the greatest of these is love" (verses 8, 13). He elevated love to the highest place of all. That's because faith and hope will be fulfilled and realized in heaven, but love will continue to be expressed in heaven through all eternity. Paul then added these simple words: "Pursue love" (1 Corinthians 14:1). Later on, he said, "Let *all* that you do be done with love" (16:14, italics added). That is, everything!

The apostle Peter wrote, "Above all things have fervent love for one another" (1 Peter 4:8). The phrase "above all things" shows love should be supreme in all that we do. Paul's foremost prayer for the Christians in Thessalonica was, "May the Lord make you *increase* and *abound* in love to one another and to all" (1 Thessalonians 3:12, italics added). When it comes to this greatest of virtues, we're to be always growing and always generous.

D. L. Moody embraced this virtue throughout his life. He practiced and preached the drawing power of love.

We need not only perseverance but we need to have love for souls. A man can succeed if only he has love for men. If we go forth simply in a professional way we will not win men, but if I can convince them that true love brings me to them, I will break down the barrier between us. This poor lost world that has swung out into the cold and the dark doesn't know anything about the love of God, and if we do not love men with the same kind of love that Jesus had for this lost world, we are not going to reach them.[19]

If this world is ever to be conquered, it will be conquered by love, and there is no way to preach love like living it in our actions.[20]

Our love shows a watching world that we belong to God. In John 13:35, Jesus told His disciples, "By this all will know that you are My disciples, if you have love for one another." And the apostle John said, "Beloved, let us love one another, for love is of God; and everyone who loves is born of God and knows God" (1 John 4:7). The display of God's love in our lives is affirmation to others that we're God's children.

We live in a world devoid of real love—the kind of love that really cares about others and puts self aside. When people see God's love through human kindness, they cannot help but be attracted to it. It's unlike worldly love, which seeks its own and has strings attached. By contrast, godly love seeks to give and expects nothing in return.

Moody speaks well of the drawing power of love in these words:

∞

To address men well they must be loved much. Whatever they may be, be they ever so guilty, or indifferent, or ungrateful, or however deeply sunk in crime, before all, and above all, they must be loved. Love is the sap of the Gospel, the secret of lively and effectual preaching, the magic power of eloquence. The end of preaching is to reclaim the hearts of men to God, and nothing but love can find out the mysterious avenues which lead to the heart. If you do not feel a fervent love and profound pity for humanity, be assured that the gift of Christian eloquence has been denied you. You will not win souls, neither will you acquire that most excellent of earthly sovereignties—sovereignty over human hearts. . . . Love is irresistible.[21]

∞

—Simple, Small Acts of Love—

It's fascinating that on Judgment Day, the test Jesus will use to separate the sheep from the goats is not related to our belief or our righteousness, but our love. The Bible teaches with absolute clarity that salvation is a free gift of God that's received by grace through faith—and not our works. Still, in Matthew 25:31–46, Jesus distinguished the sheep from the goats by the simple acts of love they performed in life—acts such as giving a cup of water, a meal, shelter, clothing, and companionship.

Moody's life was characterized by many such small kindnesses. Biographer Gamaliel Bradford wrote that "his personal kindness and consideration for others were unlimited. He was always on the lookout for those smaller helpfulnesses to friends and neighbors which go so far." [22]

R. A. Torrey, who worked alongside Moody in his evangelism and then as the superintendent and later president at what is now Moody Bible Institute, said,

> He was one of the kindest men I ever knew. He was always on the look out for kindly things to do. . . . Every morning we would find some little delicacy on our back doorstep—the first asparagus of the season, the first strawberries, or something of that sort; and we always knew where it came from. We always knew that Mr. Moody had been round before we were up;

and he, every day, would make a round of houses of relatives and friends with potatoes and asparagus and other vegetables. He did not sell these things but gave them away, simply from the kindness of his heart.[23]

In an article about Moody, fellow minister Henry Drummond said, "At the beginning of each term hundreds of students, many of them strangers, arrive to attend the seminaries [at Northfield, Massachusetts]. At such times, Mr. Moody literally haunts the depot to meet them the moment they most need a friend."[24]

Miss A. Rosie, who worked at Northfield Seminary, recalled a Thanksgiving weekend when several students, far from home and without transportation, remained on campus. "Mr. and Mrs. Moody left their own family gathering, came over to the Hall and spent two or three hours of the afternoon with us, playing games, and entering into our sports, trying to make us feel as much at home as possible."

Some students had to remain during the Christmas vacation as well. "Mr. Moody did all he could to make the time pleasant and the surroundings homelike," Rosie recalled, noting:

> The evening before Christmas word was brought that we should hang our stockings on the door handles outside of our doors. We did so, thinking perhaps it was nothing but a joke; but in the morning, when we

> brought in our stockings, we each found a card, containing Scripture appropriate for the occasion, from Mr. Moody, and a silk handkerchief from Mrs. Moody. We prized those gifts very highly, I assure you.[25]

Dwight Moody's generosity extended to bigger concerns as well. Fees for courses eventually reached $100 per term. Most couldn't raise even half their fees, and Moody usually paid the money himself or with the help of friends. For example, a staff person at Northfield once wrote a prospective student, "Do not worry about [the] financial part: I saw Mr. Moody about the matter this evening and he says you can come and have the tuition and board free. We will thank the Lord for opening the way."[26]

–Loving Your Family–

Most important of all, Moody was consistent in both the public and private sides of his life when it came to showing love for others. How often have we heard about ministry leaders who are so overcommitted outside the home that their family is neglected?

Biographer Lyle Dorsett observed, "The Moodys avoided the pitfalls that befell so many evangelists and missionaries because he and Emma made deliberate choices to be together. Making Northfield a home base ensured their having a place where the children always had relatives surrounding them."[27]

Bradford stated that "when it came to [Moody's] own children, he was inexhaustible in interest, attention, and ingenuity."[28] And *The Christian Workers Magazine* mentioned that "he never let more than a day or two pass without writing his wife and children when he was separated from them."[29]

Indeed, the depth of Moody's love for his family is particularly evident in the many letters he wrote to them. Among the more noteworthy are a heartfelt letter to his daughter before she traveled to England in 1887, and an endearing note to four-year-old granddaughter Emma Fitt on the day that the newest Moody grandchild was born.

∞

My dear Emma:

I must write you once more before you leave this land. I have news to tell you but I am real lonely at the thought of your going. It has seemed so nice to me to think of you safe and happy at Northfield. And now it seems as if a part of myself was gone and I do not know how it will seem when I get to Northfield. I need not tell you that I love you very much, far more than I can tell you, and you are in my thoughts so much of the time. I never loved you more than I do tonight. If I thought you were not going to get great good I think I should telegraph you not to go, but I know it will be a great help to you, and so I say go and may the angels of God hover over you by day and by night is my most earnest prayer. God bless you and help you and keep you will be my earnest prayer.

Your own loving father,

D. L. Moody [30]

∞

∞

My dear [granddaughter] Emma:

I am glad that you have a little cousin. Will you kiss her for me, and will you show her your grandfather's picture? I do not think she will know me, but you can tell her all about me, so she will know me when she gets older, and we will play together with her. I am going to send her a little kiss, just one by one.

Your grandfather,

D. L. Moody

I will put the kiss in a little box, O, and you can take it to her. [31]

∞

–LOVE AS OUR MOTIVE–

As we reflect on all that we do for the Lord, then, we must ask ourselves: Why am I doing this? Is it for attention? Is there some personal benefit I seek? Am I hoping to win favor in God's eyes . . . or man's? Or is it because I really love the people I'm serving? Moody often challenged his listeners to serve God for the right reasons.

If our actions are merely performed out of a sense of duty, God will not accept [those deeds]. I've heard this word duty in connection with Christian work till I am tired of it. . . . Let us strike for a higher plane—let us throw a little love into our actions, and then our services will be accepted by God if love will be the motive power.[32]

"Is love the motive power that urges us to go out and work for God?" This is the first question that we ought to ask ourselves. Without it a great deal of work will go for naught. The work will be swept away like chaff without it. Christ looks down and examines our hearts and actions, and although our deeds may be great in the eyes of the world, they may not be in His eyes.[33]

It is not always more work that we want so much as a better motive. Many of us do a good deal of work, but we must remember that God looks at the motive. The only tree on this earth that can produce fruit which is pleasing to God is the tree of love.[34]

If we desire to be successful in our ministry efforts, then it's not *what* we do that pleases God and draws men to us. Rather, it's *why* we do it. Is our service done out of love? That's what really counts.

–A Creed to Live By–

In the margin of Dwight Moody's Bible was this poignant and memorable phrase taken from elsewhere—one that would serve well as a creed for anyone who serves the Lord, especially in a leadership position:

> For our Lord Jesus Christ's sake,
>> Do all the good you can,
>> To all the people you can,
>> By all the means you can,
>> In all the places you can,
>> As long as ever you can.[35]

Love, then, is the golden thread that ought to run through all we say and do.

MOODY
from the Pulpit

GOD LOVED the world when it was full of sinners and those who broke His law. If He did so, can't we do it, and love our fellowmen? If the Saviour could die for the world, can't we work for it? . . . The churches would soon be filled if outsiders could find that people in them loved them when they came, and if the elders and deacons were glad to see them and were ready to take them by the hand and welcome them. Such things would draw sinners. Actions like these speak louder than words. We do not want to talk of love and not show it in our deeds; we want something more than tongue love.[36]

CHAPTER THREE

A Passion
for Reaching
Lost Souls

WOE IS ME IF I DO NOT
PREACH THE GOSPEL!
FOR IF I DO THIS WILLINGLY,
I HAVE A REWARD.

—1 CORINTHIANS 9:16–17

On the night of October 8, 1871, D. L. Moody finished a message with some words he regretted for the rest of his life. So great was his remorse that he committed himself to never making the same mistake again.

The title of Moody's sermon was "What Shall I Do with Jesus?" At the end he announced, "Now I want you to take the question with you and think it over, and next Sunday I want you to come back and tell me what you are going to do with Him."[1]

But next Sunday never came. As Moody dismissed his audience, the nearby courthouse firebell sounded. At the time, no one had any idea how serious the blaze would become. As it turned out, the hall in which Moody spoke, the church he established, and his home were all destroyed in the inferno that became the Great Chicago Fire, along with more than 18,000 other buildings. But Moody hardly gave a second thought to his gutted home and church. They could easily be replaced—but not the lost souls. It was the memory of the audience he never saw again that was seared in his mind for the rest of his life.

"What a mistake!" Moody later said. "Since then I never have dared give an audience a week to think of their salvation. If they were lost, they might rise up in judgment against me."[2]

William Moody explained how this affected his father's future ministry endeavors:

∞

From that time on [my father] laid great stress on the after-meeting, which took place at the close of an evangelistic address, in which he tried to bring individual souls to an immediate decision as to the great issues he had just brought before them. These meetings were probably the most characteristic and original feature of his work.[3]

∞

56

–Reaching the Lost One by One–

Before Moody came upon the scene, most speakers who held evangelistic campaigns were fairly routine in their approach: In their message they would exhort their audience to receive Christ as Savior, and at the end, people were invited to make a decision. The invitation was extended to the entire crowd, and little or nothing was done to accommodate those who might have personal questions or might need additional counsel to help lead them to the point of salvation. And seldom did any follow-up take place to ensure that those who professed new-found belief in Christ would continue on the right path and join a church.

Moody, however, knew the decision to put one's faith in the Lord Jesus Christ was a highly personal matter, and that a "one size fits all" approach of appealing to a crowd had definite limitations. He recognized every person's heart had its own set of burdens that needed to be addressed directly, and the best way for people to see their need for Christ was to see that He alone had the answers to their specific problems.

With all that in mind, Moody started what he called the "inquiry room." After a service, he would invite members of the audience to go to a nearby room where they could quietly meet one-on-one with Christian helpers who could provide guidance appropriate to each person's needs. The inquiry room allowed for highly personal interaction and opened the door for new friendships to form, making it easier for follow-up to take place in the days and weeks after a campaign.

As William Moody observed in his biography about his father,

∞

Mr. Moody was much given to the man-to-man method; he was especially interested in the inquiry-room, and always laid great stress on the necessity for competent helpers in this work. "Let every one of us try to get one soul!" was his constant appeal.[4]

∞

D. L. Moody himself said, "Personal dealing is of the most vital importance. . . . People are not usually converted under the preaching of the minister. It is in the inquiry meeting that they are most likely to be brought to Christ."[5] Another time he said,

∞

God's business is not to be done wholesale. Think of the Master Himself talking just to Nicodemus; and then how He talked to that poor woman at the well of Samaria. Christ's greatest utterances were delivered to congregations of one or two. How many are willing to speak to tens of thousands, but not to speak to a few! . . . Oh, be willing, Christians, to be built into the temple, as a polished cap-stone, or just a single brick—no matter just how, but somehow.[6]

∞

Not that Moody had a formula for those who counseled inquirers. He once stated:

> *I admit you can't lay down rules in dealing with inquirers. There are no two persons exactly alike. Matthew and Paul were a good ways apart. The people we deal with may be widely different. What would be medicine for one might be rank poison for another. In the 15th of Luke the elder son and the younger son were exactly opposite. What would have been good counsel for one might have been ruin to the other.*[7]

English minister Henry Drummond, who worked closely with Moody for two years in the United Kingdom, was greatly impressed by the effectiveness of the inquiry room, saying that "the inquiry meetings bridged the gap between the preacher and the hearer, and brought them together, man to man, before God."[8] More important, everywhere Moody went, ministers of nearby churches testified of real and lasting growth from the addition of new converts who joined their congregations. Indeed, as Moody stated, "We must have personal work—hand-to-hand work—if we are going to have results."[9]

—Enlisting Lay Believers
to Join the Work—

Connected with Moody's innovative use of the inquiry room was his equally visionary desire to equip everyday Christian men and women to minister to the inquirers. He knew it was impossible for pastors and church leaders to tend to this massive work alone, and, as he pointed out, "Christ's commission is to *every one*: 'Go ye into all the world, and preach the gospel to every creature.' If we are the branches, we are to bring forth the fruit"[10] (italics added).

Moody believed that every Christian had the potential to be used by God, and he often lamented the fact so few believers were active in reaching out to the lost.

∽

It seems to me the basest ingratitude if we do not reach out the hand to others who are down in the same pit from which we were delivered.[11]

It is a thing to weep over that we have got thousands and thousands of church members who are good for nothing towards extending the Church of God. They understand bazaars, and fairs, and sewing circles, and all that kind of work; but when you ask them to sit down and show that man or woman the way into God's kingdom, they say: "Oh, I am not able to do that. Let the deacons do it, or some one else." It is all wrong. The Church ought to be educated on this very point.[12]

One of the evidences we are children of God is, we have a desire for others; our heart will go out after others.[13]

At conferences for those who were training to become Christian workers, Moody reminded his listeners of Jesus' words that they were the light of the earth (Matthew 5:14). Every believer shares an important purpose—to bring God's light into a dark and spiritually dead world:

God has left us down here to shine. We are not here to buy and sell and get gain, to accumulate wealth, to acquire worldly position. This earth, if we are Christians, is not our home; that is up yonder. God has sent us into the world to shine for Him—to light up this dark world.[14]

To those who might object that they were too inadequate to have any kind of impact on others, Moody said, "Remember, a small light will do a good deal when it is in a very dark place. Put one little tallow candle in the middle of a large hall, and it will give a good deal of light."[15]

When it comes to introducing people to Christ, then, every little bit counts. Every believer can make a difference, no matter how seemingly small his or her contribution. Is this the encouragement you as a spiritual leader share with your followers? And are you yourself serving as an example they can emulate?

–PROCLAIMING THE MESSAGE EFFECTIVELY–

Not only did Moody attract significant attention because of his use of the inquiry room and his training of laypeople for Christian service, but also because of the unusually "ordinary" manner in which he preached.

Early in his ministry, Moody had the opportunity to visit the United Kingdom and speak at evangelistic campaigns there. When he arrived, many of the religious leaders greeted him with raised eyebrows and suspicions. What could this uneducated and unordained American possibly offer to a sophisticated and well-cultured European Christendom?

Keeping It Simple

Fortunately, Moody didn't concern himself with impressing anyone or conforming to the expectations of the religious elite, who believed in eloquence and formality in the pulpit. Instead, he proclaimed the gospel as he always had—with a refreshingly candid and heartfelt passion that thoroughly captivated his listeners. In time, those who were skeptical—including members of the press—became respectful admirers. For example, in 1873, the *Edinburgh Daily Review* declared,

> Mr. Moody is strikingly free from all pretence and parade; he speaks as one who thoroughly believes what he says and who is in downright earnest in delivering his message. His descriptions are characterized by remarkable vividness and graphic power. He has a great wealth of illustration, and his illustrations are always apposite, bringing into the clearest light the point which he intends to illustrate, and fixing it forever into the memory.[16]

A correspondent of *The Christian*, a periodical in London, said this about Moody when the evangelist spoke at the Exhibition Palace in Dublin:

> One cannot but ask the question, "What is the magic power which draws together these mighty multitudes and holds them spellbound?" Is it the worldly rank or wealth of learning or oratory of the preacher? No, for he is possessed of little of these. It is the simple lifting up of the cross of Christ—the holding forth the Lord Jesus before the eyes of the people in all the glory of His Godhead, in all the simplicity of His manhood, in all the perfection of His nature, for their admiration, for their adoration, for their acceptance.[17]

"The simple lifting up of the cross of Christ" was Moody's commitment. In a time when liberal theology was aggressively proclaiming unbiblical deviations from the gospel, Moody adhered to the gospel alone as it had always been known. While the *manner* in which Moody spoke was new and different, the *content* of his messages was the ancient and unchanging Word of God. He knew this alone had the power to change lives. Scottish pastor Andrew Thompson noted:

> There is nothing novel in the doctrine Mr. Moody proclaims. It is the old Gospel—old, and yet always fresh and young, as the living fountain or the morning sun— in which the substitution of Christ is placed in the centre and presented with admirable distinctness and decision.[18]

Moody's American audiences also appreciated his simplicity and his steadfast adherence to God's Word. For example, the *New York Tribune* stated of Moody and his coworkers, "They preach no new doctrine, no dogma of this or that sect; nothing but Christ and the necessity among us of an increased zeal in His service."[19]

And Moody himself said,

∞

Why should I get a new remedy for sin when I have found one that has never failed? The Gospel has stood the test for eighteen centuries. I know what it will do for sin-sick souls. I have tried its power for forty years.[20]

Keeping It Clear

Another strength of Moody's preaching was its remarkable clarity. Ira Sankey, a singer who accompanied D. L. Moody on all his evangelistic campaigns for more than twenty-five years and one of Dwight's closest friends, said, "One of the greatest compliments to his preaching was that the sermon that would hold the rapt attention of the most intelligent of his congregation would also be listened to with great eagerness by the children present. Any one—every one—understood what he said."[21]

Some criticized Moody for his unpolished preaching, but others differed, saying it was his very earthiness that drew the crowds and spoke most to the heart:

> Mr. Moody reaches the masses more surely and widely because he is one of them himself, and because he has not been made eloquent and faultless by the trimming and restraining processes of a liberal education. His very solecisms sound sweetly in their ears. His familiarity and conversational manner please them. They like his directness and earnestness.[22]

Especially affirming are these words written by a woman who heard Moody when she was a little child:

> As soon as Mr. Moody began to talk, I found to my surprise that I could understand him, and I liked it. He told stories—and it was Sunday too—stories when he knew people couldn't help but laugh—and then it might be a story when the grown-ups would cry. I would have cried, too, but was too busy watching this very enthusiastic preacher, who talked with his hands and feet as well as his mouth, as he paced up and down the narrow platform. No, he didn't preach, he only talked, using the simplest language, sometimes with a loud voice as he denounced wrong doing, again with tears while he pleaded for the repentance of wrong doing, but always holding the attention of his hearers.[23]

Those of us who are spiritual leaders usually have frequent opportunities to speak before others. How are we doing? Are we more concerned about impressing our audiences with our speaking skills and wisdom? Or are we keeping the message simple and clear so our listeners can understand and apply what they're hearing?

–Giving the Credit to God–

Just as a life fully surrendered to God gives God credit for any success (see pages 25–26), an effective spiritual leader recognizes he or she is merely a channel through which God does the work of drawing people and converting them. Those who were closest to Moody marveled at the fact he never exulted over the results of his ministry labors. He never took self-congratulatory glances back upon his accomplishments; rather, he was forever looking ahead, preparing for that next sermon, that next soul. This was his Master's work, not his own. Two of Moody's friends noted his intense focus in this regard:

> On the way to a prayer meeting that I knew would be crowded, though held in a large church, I remarked to him, "You must experience great pleasure in going from place to place, and reaching and benefiting such multitudes as come to hear you." He seemed scarcely to know what to say. He could not deny that he was engaged in a delightful work, but his whole mind seemed to be upon the work rather than upon his personal relations to it. I cannot recall precisely his reply. But the distinct impression left upon my mind was that this man thinks of nothing, plans for nothing but for Christ and souls.[24]

> . . .While thousands listened with intense interest to his words, he himself seemed to be forgotten—the subject, which was the Gospel always, quite covered up the speaker. And I am glad to find that, on recalling those days, it is the work itself that comes uppermost, and

the worker is almost forgotten. I marvel at it, for his personal influence was wonderful.[25]

Moody also didn't like trying to estimate how many people were won to Christ at his campaigns. Once when a minister asked him if he kept track of the numbers, Moody replied, "I don't know anything about that. . . . Thank God, I don't have to. I don't keep the Lamb's Book of Life."[26]

That Moody had a right perspective on his role in the Lord's work is also evident in this sermon excerpt:

∞

Some people come to me and say, "Mr. Moody, don't you feel a great responsibility when you come before an audience like this—don't you feel a great weight upon your shoulders?" "Well," I say, "no; I cannot convert men; I can only proclaim the Gospel."[27]

∞

–Becoming a Lasting Influence–

When Sunday school teacher Edward Kimball visited with young Dwight Moody in the back of that shoe store in Boston, he never envisioned that his casual encounter with the country boy would, in turn, lead to Moody's preaching of the gospel to many millions of people. Moody's influence also touched many special men and women who went on to become leaders, missionaries, and workers whose ministries touched many thousands of other lives.

When we reflect upon the powerful and wide-reaching ministries of people like D. L. Moody, it's easy to become disillusioned and feel that the results of our labors are insignificant by comparison. This can easily lead us to conclude that the work of soul-winning may as well be left in the hands of prominent Christian leaders who have large realms of influence. But that's not a healthy perspective to have. Winning just one soul to Christ can, in the long run, lead to the conversion of many others. The work of *every* Christian counts in this endeavor. We should never feel that winning just one soul is an insignificant thing. The spiritual leader has a passion for reaching the lost and recognizes numbers are unimportant, and even limited talents are useful in His service. Consider these thoughts from Moody:

∞

In Proverbs we read, "He that winneth souls is wise." If any man, woman, or child by a godly life and example can win one soul to God, his life will not have been a failure. He will have outshone all the mighty men of his day, because he will have set a stream in motion that will flow on and on forever and ever. [28]

If we only lead one soul to Christ we may set a stream in motion that will flow on when we are dead and gone. . . . So if you turn one to Christ, that one turned may turn a hundred; they may turn a thousand, and so the stream, small at first, goes on broadening and deepening as it rolls toward eternity.[29]

–INVITING OTHERS TO EXPERIENCE THE JOY–

While the work of sharing the gospel is not easy, it's immensely rewarding. It's the one work on earth that bears fruit we can enjoy forever in heaven. Because soul-winning is a work with eternal results, our participation in it can yield eternal satisfaction. As Moody correctly said, "It is the greatest pleasure of living to win souls to Christ."[30] And Moody, by his dedication to training up Christian workers, including little children, as the following story illustrates, made it possible for countless other believers to experience this greatest pleasure for themselves:

> It was in 1876, during the great Hippodrome meetings in New York City, that as a Christian lad I felt for the first time that there was really something that a boy could do for Jesus.
>
> Mr. Moody in a talk to personal workers said, "Every Christian should be a soul-winner"; and then, as though

looking where I sat, he added, "A Christian boy can lead other boys to Christ."

My heart gave a great leap. Could I do anything? I prayed to Jesus to help me, and said in my heart that I'd try.

That evening found me in the inquiry room, Bible in hand, and with a few verses that Mr. Moody had given us to use committed to memory. The room was full of inquirers and workers. Where could I, a mere boy, begin? Shortly, Mr. Moody came near, and I think he must have seen the longing look on my face, for putting his hand on my shoulder, he said, "There is a boy; go speak to him." And that night there came the new joy into my life of knowing I had been used to lead a soul to Jesus.[31]

If you as a spiritual leader want to lift Christian men and women upward to new levels of joy and usefulness, then you'll want to cultivate in your own life a contagious passion for souls—one that inspires others to a like passion.

MOODY
from the Pulpit

IT IS A BLESSED privilege to be used of God to bring one little lamb into the Kingdom. If we are the only means of saving one child, our life will not be a failure; we shall hear the Master's "Well done, good and faithful servant." Do you tell me there is a child of God here today who is so weak, and has so little influence that he cannot win some little child to the Master during the next week? I believe there is not a Christian now hearing me but can be instrumental in winning some soul to the Lord Jesus Christ this week if he will. That would surely be a very small thing for any one of us to do. The results of it may meet us away off on the shores of eternity.[32]

^AConstant
Readiness to Pray

CONTINUE EARNESTLY IN PRAYER,
BEING VIGILANT IN IT.

—COLOSSIANS 4:2

There's a certain saying about prayer that makes perfectly clear sense but is incredibly hard to put into practice. You may have heard variations of it before. It basically goes like this: If you take your worries or problems to God in prayer and later on are still concerned about those worries or problems, then you didn't really release them into God's hands.

Many are familiar with 1 Peter 5:7, which says to "cast all your anxiety on him because he cares for you" (NIV). Philippians 4:6, another well-known passage, tells us to "be anxious for nothing," but to "let your requests be made known to God." And what does God promise to give us when we truly place our requests in His hands? "The *peace* of God . . . will guard your hearts and minds through Christ Jesus" (verse 7, italics added).

Yet how often do we fail to truly yield our burdens to the Lord? How many times have we offered a crisis or concern to Him in prayer, only to let it gnaw at us again afterward? As Moody demonstrates, spiritual leaders find power and peace by visiting with God regularly in prayer.

–PEACE IN THE MIDST OF PREDICAMENTS–

Given the enormous load of responsibilities D. L. Moody had upon his shoulders, he could have easily become overwhelmed on many occasions. At numerous times he and his coworkers didn't know how they would meet the financial obligations of the schools, or how they would work out all the demanding details of setting up a citywide campaign. They experienced many moments of uncertainty, not knowing *how* their dilemma would be solved.

But what Moody did know was *who* to turn to in these predicaments. It was at times like these that Moody exhibited the remarkable depth of trust he possessed in his heavenly Father. He knew that no crisis ever caught God by surprise, and that if it was God's will for a need to be met, it would be met. So after he prayed about a matter, he ceased to let it bother him. While he might continue to offer the same prayer to the Lord out of earnestness, he knew there was no sense in allowing the problem itself to make him anxious. It was this complete and childlike trust that enabled Moody to keep moving forward productively in his work, unencumbered by the distractions of worries.

Fellow minister Major Whittle observed, "His prayers while I was with him were as simple as a child's full of trust, humility, and expectation that God would not disappoint him. There seemed to be an understanding established between the servant and the Master which made long prayers or the importunity of repetition unnecessary."[1]

Dr. R. A. Torrey, an associate of Moody's at the Chicago Bible Institute (now Moody Bible Institute, [MBI]), recalled one time when they both were concerned about an issue. Moody drove up in his carriage and asked Torrey to accompany him.

> We drove along by the bank of a brook amid overhanging maples. By this brook we stopped, and Mr. Moody said, "Let us pray." Like a child he went and walked into his Father's presence, and told him all about our troubles, and then took up the reins and drove on, perfectly triumphant and perfectly unconcerned, knowing that the battle was won. He knew that God was a God that answers prayer.[2]

At a conference several months after Moody's death, one speaker reminisced about how Mr. Moody overcame difficulties through prayer. "When great and apparently insurmountable difficulties rose in any path he was pursuing, . . . often he would say, 'Let us take this to God in prayer.' Then . . . he [easily] led us all into God's very presence, and with . . . mighty power of simplicity and faith he took hold upon God."[3]

In these observations by Torrey and the conference speaker are some key traits worth nothing. First, Moody viewed God as a caring Father eager to hear His children's requests. Second, his prayers were spontaneous. When a need or burden arose, he prayed. And third, most important of all, he really did release his concerns heavenward. After he prayed about a matter, he left it in God's hands, fully confident that the Lord had full control over the situation and would answer according to His wisdom and will. *That's* trust!

–The Habit of Prayer–

That Moody sought his heavenly Father automatically in times of need is most likely a reflection of the fact that prayer was part and parcel of his everyday life. For him, prayer was a habit—an ongoing part of all he did. He began each day in prayer, and lived all through each day in a spirit of readiness to pray.

His son William noted that during the summer Moody typically rose about daybreak for his "quiet season alone with his Bible and his God, while his mind was fresh, and before the activities of the day divided his attention."[4] William believed the tone "was one of constant communion with God." Therefore, "It was not surprising . . . that [my father] should seldom have long seasons of agonizing prayer such as some have experienced, for his closeness to God was not limited to special seasons, but was a continuous and uninterrupted service."[5]

James M. Gray, who became the second president of MBI, concluded that "Mr. Moody's life was a life of prayer. He was always in the spirit of prayer. I do not suppose there was anything in his life concerning which he did not ask God."[6]

Moody's view of God had a definite impact on the kind of relationship he enjoyed with the Lord.

> To Mr. Moody God was not a mere law or abstraction. To him God was a Person who feels and thinks, a Father who rules and loves and is concerned with everything which affects His children. With this conception of God, we are not surprised to find Mr. Moody leading a life of ceaseless communion with Him, out of which grew a life of overcoming strength.[7]

> Moody speaks of God and to God as if He were a man around the corner, who could be addressed and touched like a real human friend.[8]

Cultivating this kind of prayer life, of course, requires discipline, both in terms of time and attention. It requires developing a habit of coming to God regularly and getting to know Him more personally through His Word. The more we are with Him and the better we know Him, the more intimate our relationship with Him will become and the more meaningful our prayer life will be.

As you consider the traits that marked Moody's prayer life—his view of God as a caring Father and friend, his spontaneity, his complete trust, his full dependence, his intimate communion—do you see where you can grow in your own prayer life? Might more diligence in prayer bring you to the point where this spiritual discipline becomes a more natural and ongoing extension of all that you do?

—THE NECESSITY OF PRAYER—

Moody also believed firmly in a connection between a leader's prayer life and the effectiveness of his ministry. He observed that Jesus prayed during His baptism, before His transfiguration, before His crucifixion, and before choosing the disciples. If the Son of God Himself found it desirable to pray before or during the momentous events of His life, then should we be any different? Moody went on to conclude, "My friends, if we are going to do a great work for God, we must spend much time in prayer; we have got to be closeted with God."[9]

Moody also believed that a significant part of a leader's success had to do with the prayers of his people:

∞

I have noticed, in traveling up and down the country, and after mingling with a great many ministers, that it is not the man that can preach the best that is the most successful, but the man who knows how to get his people together to pray.[10]

If the man who is your minister preaches the gospel, you stand by him; pray for him. What a help it is for a man that is preaching to have a lot of people in the pews praying for him.[11]

∞

–THE QUESTIONS ABOUT PRAYER–

Because of Moody's frequent exhortations to believers about their need to commune with God regularly, it was inevitable that people would ask him, "But what about the times when I do pray and God doesn't answer? Why won't He respond?"

First, Moody pointed out that even when we're unsure of how God might answer, we're still commanded to bring our requests to Him:

∞

*Some of you may have wondered what good it will
do to make these requests for prayer. But the Lord
tells us that we are to make our requests known.
People say, "Does God answer prayer?" Well, He says
so, and I will take His word for it. Now, my friends,
let us call upon Him; He has told us to do it.*[12]

∞

Sometimes, though, it seems that our prayers are being ignored.
In his messages, Moody suggested some questions we might
ask ourselves when our prayers seem to go unanswered.

Are your prayers according to God's will?

When we pray, it's good to remember God has a bird's-eye view
of the entire world as well as the future, and He knows how to
orchestrate all things so that ultimately they conform to His
sovereign plan for all time. By contrast, we view all of life from
the trenches. All we can see is the immediate moment. We
don't know what's going to happen the next day, the next
week, the next month. So, when we pray, it's possible we may
unknowingly present a request that stands at odds with God's
plans for the future. That's why, when we bring a petition to
Him, we want to qualify it by subjecting it to His will.

∞

*Now if we have spread our requests before the Lord,
then just say, "Thy will be done." . . . Keep that in*

mind. We very often set our will against God's. That will be our ruin, perhaps. Let the will of God be done. I cannot look a day into the future, and I would not dare to take the responsibility. It is far better for us to say, "Thy will, not mine, be done."[13]

In true prayer there will be submission. Just make your request to God, and say, "Thy will be done, not mine." The sweetest lesson I have learned is to let God choose for me in temporal things.[14]

This principle of leaving matters in the Lord's hand and subjecting ourselves to His will is well illustrated in this engaging story about Moody's offer to buy a doll for his daughter:

I learned a lesson once from my little girl. She was always teasing me for a great big doll. She had a lot of dolls around the house without heads, some without arms, some without legs, but she wanted a great big doll. You know if a man has an only daughter he is rather soft (and they find it out, you know); so she was determined to get that big doll. One day I had a good streak come over me, and I took her to a toyshop to get her a doll, but as we went in the door we saw a basket of little china dolls. "O papa, isn't that the

cutest little doll you ever saw?" "Yes, yes." "Well, won't you buy it?" "Well, now, Emma, let me choose this time." "O, no, papa; I just want this little doll."

I paid a nickel for the doll and took her home. After the newness had worn off, the doll was left with all the others. I said, "Emma, do you know what I was going to do that day when I took you into the toyshop, and you selected that little china doll?" "No, papa." "Well, I was going to buy you one of those great big ones." "You were? Why didn't you do it?" "Because you wouldn't let me. You remember you wanted that little doll, and you would have it." The little thing saw the point, and she bit her lips and did not say anything more. From that day to this I cannot get her to say what she wants. When I was going to Europe the last time, I asked her what she wanted me to bring her, and she said, "Anything you like."

*I*t is far better to let God choose for us than to choose for ourselves. "Thy will, not mine, be done."[15]

∞

Are your prayers in line with God's best for you?
God knows what needs to happen today in our lives in order for us to enjoy His best for us tomorrow. Thus, if we make a request that might prevent His good work from being done

in our lives, then He will either refrain from fulfilling that request, or may at least postpone fulfilling it. When God denies a request for the moment, it's most likely because He has something better in store for us. As Moody said,

∞

God knows what we want better than we do, in temporal things. God loves us too well. There was Paul. He prayed and prayed earnestly that God would take the thorn out of his flesh. But God said: "That will do, Paul; I cannot do it. The thorn must remain; it will give you more grace." Then Paul thanked God for the thorn. He wouldn't have it out if he could, because he got more grace by it. These things bring us closer to Christ.[16]

Many are asking for what would be an injury to them should God grant it. . . . He knows when anything would injure us, should we have it, and it is because He loves us that many prayers are unanswered. We sometimes fail to see why God withholds certain gifts, but later in life we will understand it.[17]

∞

Are your prayers being hampered by sin?

God takes sin seriously—so much so that, when we entertain its presence in our lives, He refuses to hear our prayers, according to Psalm 66:18: "If I regard iniquity in my heart, the Lord will not hear." And, lest we rationalize that surely the "lesser" sins of life don't really affect our communion with God, we need to remember that all sin—no matter how small—is an affront to His perfect holiness.

It is impossible for us to embrace both sin and God at the same time, for He is "of purer eyes than to behold evil, and cannot look on wickedness" (Habakkuk 1:13). In fact, for God to accept our devotions while we continue to harbor sin in our hearts makes Him tolerant of that sin. The psalmist had the right perspective about approaching God when he asked, "Who may ascend into the hill of the Lord? Or who may stand in His holy place? He who has clean hands and a pure heart" (Psalm 24:3–4).

As Moody said,

∞

God delights to answer prayer. But you cannot deceive yourself. If you are living a dishonorable life, God hides His face, and will not hear you.[18]

If there is anything in your life which you know to be wrong, do not sleep until you have the thing settled with God, and you will get the greatest blessing you have ever had on earth. God delights to give gifts to the sons of men. "He that spared not his own Son, but delivered him up for us all, how shall he not with him also freely give us all things?" [Romans 8:32 KJV]. [19]

There is no true prayer without confession. As long as we have unconfessed sin in our soul we are not going to have power with God in prayer. He says if we regard iniquity in our hearts He will not hear us, much less answer. As long as we are living in any known sin, we have no power in prayer. God is not going to hear it. [20]

–OUR PERSISTENCE IN PRAYER–

There may be times when, after we've offered a request many times over, we still don't get an answer from God. Does that mean we should give up? Not necessarily. As mentioned earlier, while God sometimes says no because our request does not line up with His will or it's not His best for us, there's also the possibility that God's timeline for fulfilling the request is different than ours. He may have reasons for delaying the response. Because He is all-knowing and we aren't, we need to willingly acquiesce to His timing when it comes to answering our prayers. Moody had this to say regarding perseverance in prayer:

Now, I don't like to be teased; I suppose you don't. I don't know why, but somehow or other the Lord seems to like it. He likes to have us press our cause, and what we want is to pray on and never faint. There is no gauge to God's promises. You may pray for weeks, months, or years; you may go down to your grave, and your prayers may not all be answered, but perhaps around your coffin that wayward boy may be converted. We are instructed to pray and never cease. Pray right on. And if we get discouraged, we are disobeying God, and are not doing what the Lord would like to have us do.[21]

–FULFILLING YOUR PART IN PRAYER–

While it's true that in the act of prayer we're to express complete trust in God and yield to whatever His will might be, that doesn't mean we are to remain passive in relation to our prayer requests. For example, when we pray for a person's salvation, it's appropriate for us to also act upon whatever opportunities we might have to share the gospel with that person. Or, when we pray for God to provide for someone and meet a need, if we can be part of meeting that need, we are to take action. Moody, for example, prayed alongside many of his school students for God to provide the financial means for them to attend the school—and then Moody made himself a part of the answer by reaching into his own pocket and paying for part of the fees. That's what Moody meant by this slogan he had about prayer:

∞

Pray as though everything depended upon God but work as though everything depended upon you.[22]

∞

–THE POWER OF PRAYER–

Without question, one of the more significant legacies left by D. L. Moody is the school now known as Moody Bible Institute in the city of Chicago. The school, now more than one hundred years old and still thriving, has trained tens of thousands of men and women to carry on the work of ministry in countries all over the globe. And students at the school today continue to reach out to people in the more destitute districts of the city—just as their founder did. Through the years, MBI's students and influence have also given birth to literally hundreds of other Christian schools and organizations and programs that are involved in evangelism, pastoral training, missions, publishing Christian literature, and much more. All told, it's safe to say that literally millions of lives have been touched through the years by those who received their training at MBI.

It all began, of course, with prayer. Dr. Charles Goss was with Moody when the evangelist first shared with him his plans to start the Bible school in Chicago:

> One day while I was riding with him in his buggy in Northfield, he drove up a beautiful and quiet valley and began to talk about his plans. His eyes kindled and his face glowed. Suddenly he stopped the horse, took off his hat, and said in tones that sent a positive physical thrill through me, "I am awfully concerned about this matter. Let us pray God to help us consecrate ourselves to it." That prayer went up to heaven if any thing ever did.[23]

Moody put his vision and plans in the best place possible— in God's hands. He knew that if this school was to become reality and enjoy true success, only God could make it happen. This is the pattern we find behind all the work Moody did for the Lord, both before and after the establishment of MBI. Moody would prayerfully submit the matter to God, seeking His good and perfect will, and then he would actively move forward in fulfilling his vision for as long as he could discern that God was leaving the doors of opportunity open for him.

In all we do as spiritual leaders, may that serve as an example for us. May we have a constant readiness to pray, placing our every endeavor in the Lord's hands. May our communion with God remain constant so we are sensitive to His leading in every area of our lives. And may we remember to pray with pure hearts, so that the Lord may respond to our petitions in accordance to His will and His best for our lives.

MOODY
from the Pulpit

YOU NEVER GET more than one day's journey from Christ if you come to Him every morning. Shut the world out. Get closeted with God and you will learn His secrets. I like to get up at five o'clock in the morning and turn the key and be alone, and let God talk with me. Some people say, "I cannot concentrate my thoughts. My mind just goes all over the world." Well, that is true. There is no bigger tramp on the earth than the human mind. Some of you are off in Africa now; some of you may be going to the moon and off to the stars. It is astonishing how the mind travels, and you ask, How can we bring our thoughts into captivity and have fellowship with God, instead of thinking of ourselves and everything under the sun? Prayer is important; but there is something else as important. When I pray I am talking to God; when I read the Bible God talks to me. We need both. They help us to bring our thoughts into captivity.[24]

A
Dependence
Upon the
Spirit's Power

BE FILLED WITH THE SPIRIT.
—EPHESIANS 5:18

What was the secret to D. L. Moody's success?

In the season of retrospection and reminiscence that inevitably follows the death of a great leader, this question must have arisen again and again, for R. A. Torrey, who worked closely with Moody and became superintendent of what would become the Moody Bible Institute, frequently spoke and wrote on this very issue.

For example, in an article titled "D. L. Moody: Lessons from His Life and Death," Torrey wrote, "The whole secret of Mr. Moody's influence and effectiveness can be put into one word, and that word is power. But whence this power? The enduement with the Holy Spirit."[1] And in a message at the first Northfield conference after Moody's homegoing, Torrey stated,

> "What is the secret of that man's success?" many have asked me. One of the easiest questions that could be asked. *He had power.* But where did he get that strange power by which he swayed the affections and wills of men? He knew, and we may all know. It was the Holy Ghost upon him.[2]

"He worked in the power of the Holy Spirit," Torrey later wrote in *The Institute Tie*, predecessor of the classic *Moody* magazine. "When the Spirit of God put it in his heart to do something, he acted immediately. He knew the Holy Spirit as a living Person. The one impression more than anything else that I have of him, is the Holy Ghost power in his life."[3]

Moody's acknowledgment of the Holy Spirit's role in his ministry was significant. The doctrine of the Holy Spirit was actively taught at all Moody's schools and at his Northfield conferences. In addition, at the conferences Moody passionately exhorted all the attendees to seek the Spirit's filling in their lives. Moody felt the church in general gave too little attention to the Holy Spirit, and more importantly, Moody asserted that if anyone wanted to be effective in ministry, he must receive empowerment from the Spirit. In the preface of his book titled *Secret Power* (published in 1881), Moody said the Holy Spirit "has been too much overlooked, as though it were not practical, and the result is lack of power in testimony and work."

−SEEKING THE SPIRIT'S POWER−

Unfortunately, there was and continues to be much misunderstanding as to exactly what Moody taught about the Holy Spirit. As we consider his thoughts regarding this member of the Trinity, let's keep in mind that his lack of formal theological training sometimes meant he wasn't precise in his definitions or his use of certain terms. As a result, some people—both in Moody's time and in our day—have arrived at erroneous conclusions about Moody's views on the Spirit.

The most common misperception is that Moody advocated a second conversion experience. But as Stanley Gundry points out, "This is terminology that Moody never used and which expresses a concept in direct contradiction to what he preached . . . he described it as a filling, a baptism, or an anointing."[4]

The Spirit Indwells All Believers

Although we might find ourselves somewhat uncertain about a few aspects of what Moody taught about the Spirit, upon carefully examining all his teachings, we find confirmation that he was consistent on two crucial points. First, he recognized the Bible's teaching (see Romans 8:9; Ephesians 1:13–14) that all believers are indwelt by the Spirit:

∞

I think it is clearly taught in Scripture that every believer has the Holy Ghost dwelling in him. He may be quenching the Spirit of God, and he may not glorify God as he should, but if he is a believer on the Lord Jesus Christ, the Holy Ghost dwells in him. I believe today, that though Christian men and women have the Holy Spirit dwelling in them, yet He is not dwelling within them in power.[5]

The Spirit Fills Believers Who Yield

Second, Moody recognized the biblical distinction between the *indwelling* of the Spirit and the *filling* of the Spirit (or what he also referred to as the baptism of the Spirit or the anointing of the Spirit). Although this distinction is correct from a scriptural point of view, Moody's reference to the *filling* and the *baptism* of the Spirit as synonymous is questionable. It seems more appropriate to see the baptism of the Spirit as synonymous with the indwelling rather than the filling, based on 1 Corinthians 12:13, which says, "By one Spirit we were all baptized into one body"—a clear reference to the miracle of indwelling that happens at the moment of salvation. But Moody did correctly see the indwelling as a once-for-all event that took place at salvation, and the filling as a complete yieldedness to the Spirit's power and control. He believed that as Christians we are all indwelt by the Spirit, and that we are commanded to always live in a state of yieldedness that permits the Spirit to work in and through us—which, biblically speaking, is what it means to "be filled with the Spirit" (Ephesians 5:18).

Here's what Moody said:

∞

There is a difference between the indwelling of the Holy Ghost and His filling one with power. Every true child of God, who has been cleansed by the blood of Christ, is a temple or dwelling-place of the Holy Ghost. But yet he may not have fullness of power.[6]

We read in Ephesians 5:18 that this is a command: "Be filled with the Spirit." God commands us to be filled with the Spirit; and if we are not filled, it is because we are living beneath our privileges. I think that is the great trouble with Christendom today: we are not living up on the plane where God would have us live.[7]

∞

It's helpful to consider, in Moody's own words, what prompted his great emphasis on the Spirit in his ministry. As he reported it, while in New York in 1871, he sought and received this blessing:

∞

I was crying all the time that God would fill me with His Spirit. Well, one day, in the city of New York— oh, what a day!—I cannot describe it, I seldom refer to it; it is almost too sacred an experience to name. . . . I can only say that God revealed Himself to me, and I had such an experience of His love that I had to ask Him to stay His hand. I went to preaching again. The sermons were not different; I did not present any new truths, and yet hundreds were converted. I would not now be placed back where I was before that blessed experience if you should give me all the world—it would be as the small dust of the balance.[8]

There are two epochs in my life which stand out clear. One is when I was between 18 and 19 years old, when I was born *of the Spirit. . . . The greatest blessing, next to being born again, came 16 years after, when I was* filled *with the Spirit*[9] [emphasis added].

Again, Moody sometimes didn't define his thoughts with the greatest theological precision. Yet we cannot help but agree that the Bible does urge us to do the work of ministry in the Spirit's power and not our own. The apostle Paul exhorted us to be filled with the Spirit (Ephesians 5:18) and to walk in the Spirit (Galatians 5:16). Both commands, which appear in the present tense in the original Greek text, speak of an ongoing, continuous replenishment or a habitual pattern of life. We are to continually submit ourselves moment by moment so the Spirit can do His work through us. This is not a passive submission, but an active one, in which we are urged to serve as a good soldier, compete as an athlete, exert the diligence of a hardworking farmer (see 2 Timothy 2:3–6), and to "run with endurance the race that is set before us" (Hebrews 12:1).

Moody's longing for himself and his constant plea to his fellow believers—particularly ministry workers—was that they always yield themselves as instruments through which the Spirit could work unimpeded, lest they become useless to God:

I believe the reason why God makes use of so few in the Church, is because there is not in them the power that God can use. He is not going to use our ideas, but we must have the Word of God hid in our hearts, and then, the Holy Spirit inflaming us, we will have the testimony which will be rich, and sweet, and fresh, and the Lord's Word will vindicate itself in blessed results. God wants to use us; God wants to make us channels of blessing; but we are in such a condition He does not use us.[10]

–Benefiting from the Spirit's Power–

Considering it is the Spirit who is our helper, our teacher, and our guide, there's no question we're infinitely better off when we rely on His empowerment and not our own feeble resources. Moody, in his messages about the Holy Spirit, spoke of at least two ways we benefit from His power.

Our Work Is Made Easier

Because the Holy Spirit has supernatural power and always works in full harmony with God's will, we will find our work of ministry much easier when we depend upon His leading. We won't find ourselves inadvertently going against the grain of God's desires for us.

How easy it is to work for God when we are filled with His Spirit! His service is so sweet, so delightful; He is not a hard master. People talk about their being overworked and breaking down. It is not so. It is [over-worry] and care that wears people out.[11]

Why do so many workers break down? Not from overwork, but because there has been friction of the machinery; there hasn't been enough of the oil of the Spirit. Great engines have their machinery so arranged that where there is friction there is oil dropping on it all the time. It is a good thing for Christians to have plenty of oil.[12]

Without this power, our work will be drudgery. With it, it becomes a joyful task, a refreshing service.[13]

Our Teaching Is More Effective

Moody also pointed out that our preaching and teaching are positively affected when we are filled with the Spirit and walking with Him. In John 14:26, Jesus said the Holy Spirit "will teach you all things," and in John 15:26 He said the Spirit "will testify of Me." Thus, the Spirit is our teacher. As such, wouldn't it make sense that we, who are imperfect human vessels, depend upon the Spirit's perfect power and guidance? Here are some of the connections Moody made between the Spirit and our speaking ministry:

Our Gospel that we are preaching is a supernatural Gospel, and we have got to have supernatural power to preach it.[14]

If a man is not filled with the Spirit, he will never know how to use the Book. We are told that this is the sword of the Spirit; and what is an army good for that does not know how to use its weapons?[15]

The Gospel proclamation can not be divorced from the Holy Spirit. Unless He attend the word in power, vain will be the attempt in preaching it. Human eloquence or persuasiveness of speech are the mere trappings of the dead, if the living Spirit be absent.[16]

Indeed, without the illumining help of the Spirit, we would not be able to understand the Scriptures, much less be able to teach them to others.

–Receiving the Spirit's Power–

In chapter 1, as we discovered the importance of living in full surrender to God, we saw that the presence of sin in our lives will block God's ability to work through us. In the same way, when we harbor sin within us, we hinder the Spirit's ability to use us. We must empty ourselves of self; our yieldedness is the channel through which the Spirit's power can flow. Thus Moody declared:

I believe firmly, that the moment our hearts are emptied of pride and selfishness and ambition and self-seeking, and everything that is contrary to God's law, the Holy Ghost will come and fill every corner of our hearts; but if we are full of pride and conceit,

and ambition and self-seeking, and pleasure and the world, there is no room for the Spirit of God; and I believe many a man is praying to God to fill him, when he is full already with something else. Before we pray that God would fill us, I believe we ought to pray Him to empty us.[17]

Remember, He is not going to give this power to an impatient man; He is not going to give it to a selfish man; He will never give it to an ambitious man whose aim is selfish, till first emptied of self; emptied of pride and of all worldly thoughts. Let it be God's glory and not our own that we seek, and when we get to that point, how speedily the Lord will bless us for good. Then will the measure of our blessing be full.[18]

That we can only be filled with self or filled with the Spirit—and not both at the same time—is affirmed in Galatians 5:16–17: "Walk in the Spirit, and you shall not fulfill the lust of the flesh. For the flesh lusts against the Spirit, and the Spirit against the flesh; and these are contrary to one another." Moody echoed this truth as well:

∞

If a man is filled with the Holy Spirit . . . then there is no room for the world, then there is no room for self, then there is no room for unholy ambitions and unholy desires, then there is no room for self-seeking and lauding self; but a man will have the mind that Christ had, when he is filled with that Spirit.[19]

∞

What is your state of yieldedness right now? You cannot live partially submitted to self and partially submitted to the Spirit at the same time. Either you yield the throne of your heart completely to the Spirit's control, or not at all. As Moody said, may we ask God to reveal what we need to empty from ourselves before we ask the Spirit to fill and empower us.

–PURSUING THE SPIRIT'S POWER–

As noted earlier, the Bible's commands for us to remain filled with the Spirit and to walk in the Spirit indicate that we're to continuously seek His empowerment in our lives. The call to live in total yieldedness never ends. We cannot assume that because we once submitted ourselves fully to the Spirit that we'll be adequately empowered for all future ministry endeavors. As still-imperfect humans, we do at times surrender our thoughts and actions to the desires of the flesh, and thus find ourselves in a position of needing to empty ourselves of sin and self before we can once again be filled.

∞

The fact is, we are leaky vessels, and we have to keep right under the fountain all the time to keep full of Christ, and so have fresh supply.[20]

I believe this is a mistake a great many of us are making; we are trying to do God's work with the grace God gave us ten years ago. We say, if it is necessary, we will go on with the same grace. Now, what we want is a fresh supply, a fresh anointing and fresh power, and if we seek it, and seek it with all our hearts, we will obtain it.[21]

∞

As Moody once said, "Let us not forget that all strength and help has come from on high."[22] The moment we begin to credit our ministry results to our genius, our skills, our knowledge, we immediately unplug ourselves from the true power source of all effective ministry—the Holy Spirit. We can sometimes get away with this for a while, as the momentum gained over a cumulative period of ministry doesn't usually come to an abrupt stop. And though we might spiral downward gradually, we will definitely continue downward. We'll discover a loss of power because we'll find ourselves attempting to accomplish supernatural work through natural strength. Simply put, that's impossible to do. Only the Holy Spirit's power can miraculously enliven our words and actions to touch and change the lives of others.

As spiritual leaders, then, may we always live in total dependence upon the Spirit—a pursuit that dovetails beautifully with our need to live in total surrender to God. Then, and only then, will we know the fullness of what God desires to achieve in our lives.

MOODY
from the Pulpit

WHEN I WAS OUT in California, the first time I went down from the Sierra Nevada Mountains and dropped into the Valley of the Sacramento, I was surprised to find on one farm that everything about it was green—all the trees and flowers, everything was blooming, . . . and just across the hedge everything was dried up, and there was not a green thing there. I could not understand it. I made inquiries, and I found that the man that had everything green, irrigated; he just poured the water right on, and kept everything green, while the fields that were next to his were as dry as Gideon's fleece without a drop of dew. So it is with a great many in the church today. They are like these farms in California—a dreary desert, everything parched and desolate, and apparently no life in them. They can sit next to a man who is full of the Spirit of God, who is like a green bay tree, and who is bringing forth fruit, and yet they will not seek a similar blessing.

Well, why this difference? Because God has poured water on him that was thirsty; that is the difference. One has been seeking this anointing, and he has received it; and when we want this above everything else God will surely give it to us.[23]

CHAPTER SIX

A Dedication To God's Word

PREACH THE WORD! BE READY
IN SEASON AND OUT OF SEASON.
CONVINCE, REBUKE, EXHORT,
WITH ALL LONGSUFFERING
AND TEACHING.

—2 TIMOTHY 4:2

If the quality of your spiritual leadership were compared to a water well, how would you rate?

Back in pioneer days, digging a water well was hard work. It meant breaking through hard layers of rock to reach the water table, however deep it might be. This required weeks, if not months, of digging. Once water began seeping into the well, that wasn't the end of the work. Then came the matter of drawing the water to the surface, usually with the help of a rope and bucket or a pump—a tiring ritual that had to be performed day after day, week after week, month after month. If the well ran dry, sometimes the hole had to be dug deeper. Those who used the well also had to be careful to avoid removing water at a rate faster than nature could supply it.

There was also the ongoing task of keeping the water clean. If small animals fell into the well and died, the water would become contaminated. These had to be removed, as well as rotting leaves and insects that might have fallen in. If the well had been lined with wood to keep the sides from caving in, then moss and algae would grow on the wood near the water's edge. The wood could also cause tannic acid buildup in the water. Cleaning a well was dirty and unpleasant work, but an absolute necessity if the users didn't want to lose their source of life-giving sustenance.

In many ways, a spiritual leader is like a water well. When we pour out spiritual nourishment to others, we must take care to replenish the supply, or we'll soon have nothing to offer. We can't give what we don't have. We're also responsible for making sure the water we dispense is clean—a reminder that if our lives have become dirtied in some way, we could end up harming others.

–DRINKING SPIRITUAL WATER–

The water we give out, of course, comes from the Bible. The more we drink in from God's Word in our own life, the more we can pour out to others. And the more vigilant we are about preventing our human selves from contaminating that water, the more effective our ministry will be.

And yes, diligence is required on our part to draw upon the water of the Word day after day, week after week, month after month. It's a labor that's constant, for the needs of the people around us are constant. Their growth, in part, depends upon our growth. When we take the time to ensure our lives abound with spiritual water, their lives are more likely to abound with spiritual fruit.

Dwight Moody understood this principle, saying,

∞

A preacher, if he wants to give his people the Word, must have fed on the Word himself. A man must get water out of a well when there is water. He may dip his bucket in if it is empty, but he will get nothing. . . . So, my friends, if we attempt to feed others we must first be fed ourselves.[1]

∞

−An Unceasing Learner−

As a speaker, Moody had an abundance to offer to his listeners. During the course of a campaign, it was not unusual for him to speak as many as ten times a week. Through his many years of ministry, his impact never diminished—thanks to his habit of rising early in the morning to spend time in the Word. Indeed, R. A. Torrey attributed Moody's power to being "a deep and practical student of the Bible" whom God could use. Moody told Torrey, "If I am going to get in any study, I have got to get up before the other folks get up."[2]

Fellow Bible teacher Charles R. Erdman added,

> Moody studied his Bible. A good many of us who praise the Bible and speak in great terms of what the Bible does and can do, do not know the Bible very well. He studied his Bible. If we are correctly informed he would rise three hours before breakfast, to be alone in that study with his Bible and his Lord, patiently, devotedly seeking to understand the Scriptures as the Word of God. Some tell us he did not have a critical apparatus and scholarly method, but he came to know the Word; he came to understand the characters, doctrines, great realities of this book and that was only possible by diligent and faithful study.[3]

So great was Moody's hunger for understanding the Scriptures that he eagerly took advantage of every opportunity to learn from his more knowledgeable peers. In fact, one of the reasons he desired to make his first trip to the United Kingdom was to sit and learn from gifted teachers, such as Charles Spurgeon and Andrew Bonar. Also, anytime Moody invited prominent ministers to speak at his campaigns or conferences, he would sit in the front row of the audience and listen earnestly to his guests with a notebook in hand.

> He used to say it was worth going a thousand miles to get a good thought. With what keenness he listened to other preachers for good thoughts and illustrations, and how his face lit up as he took out the notebook which he kept in his hip-pocket! He urged this habit of making notes of all the good things one read and heard, believing that it would make the Bible more deeply interesting day by day.[4]

Whenever Moody found himself in the company of fellow preachers, he was sure to ask them their thoughts on certain Bible truths and passages. He felt no embarrassment in this; he saw no shame in humbly assuming the role of an inquiring student among his peers. Here is the spiritual leader as a life-long learner. Moody's attitude toward always gleaning truth from the Scriptures is one all of us should have, considering the fact the Bible contains an infinitely inexhaustible wealth of truth for us to learn.

Lifelong friend D. W. McWilliams described one of Moody's interactions that took place with a group of ministers:

> On being introduced to those present Mr. Moody soon turned to one of the ministers and said, "How do you

explain this verse in the Bible?" giving the verse in full. Soon after he turned to another minister, quoted a verse, and asked, "What does that mean?" The entire conversation that day was exposition of Scripture in reply to Mr. Moody's rapid questions, and a stirring of hearts in the direction of personal work for the salvation of others. The impression made upon the guests that day was of Mr. Moody's love for the souls of others and his intense desire for Bible knowledge.[5]

Oh, that we might always possess a similar enthusiasm for learning!

–Some Practical Exhortations–

When it came to reading and learning the Bible, Moody practiced what he preached. His encouragements for people —including fellow leaders—to immerse themselves in the Scriptures were not empty words. Notice, too, his emphasis upon quality of study rather than quantity.

∞

If you are a preacher or a Sunday-school teacher try at any cost to master your Bible. You ought to know it better than any one in your congregation or class.[6]

The reason why we have so little success in our teaching is because we know so little of the Word of God.

You must know it, and have it in your heart. A great many have it in their head and not in their heart.[7]

Set apart at least fifteen minutes a day for study and meditation. This little time will have great results and will never be regretted.[8]

Learn at least one verse of the Scripture each day. Verses committed to memory will be wonderfully useful in your daily life and walk. "Thy word I have hid in mine heart, that I might not sin against thee." Some Christians can quote Shakespeare and Longfellow better than the Bible.[9]

Read the Bible, my friends, as if you were seeking for something of value. It is a good deal better to take a single chapter, and spend a month on it, than to read the Bible at random for a month.[10]

Only when we as leaders are constant in the quality intake of God's Word can we give out instruction and counsel that truly satisfies the spiritual hunger of those around us.

I believe the reason people won't come more than they do into our churches is because we don't feed them enough on the Word of God. They have been

fed on sawdust long enough. . . . Go into one of our city parks in winter to feed the birds and throw down a handful of sawdust. You may deceive them once, but you won't a second time. But throw down crumbs, and they'll sweep them up. So in the churches, give people the Word of God and they will know the difference.[11]

∞

And, the more intimately we know the Scriptures, the more we make it possible for God to use us:

∞

If we want to understand it we've got to study it— read it on our knees, asking the Holy Ghost to give us the understanding to see what the word of God is, and if we go about it that way . . . we will soon know our Bible, and when we know our Bible then it is that God can use us.[12]

∞

In light of all this, we can see why it's vital for us to zealously guard our time alone with the Bible. Clearly, Scripture is to be our priority as we fulfill our responsibilities as spiritual leaders. One evening after a large meeting, while Moody walked home with Major Whittle, the latter asked a question that prompted Moody to open his Bible to 2 Timothy 4:2 and say, "'Preach the word; be instant in season, out of season; reprove, rebuke, exhort with all longsuffering and doctrine (KJV).' . . . This is our commission, Whittle."[13]

Are we living up to this commission?

–A PROFOUND EFFECTIVENESS–

As a preacher and teacher of God's Word, Moody's approach was rather simple. He made the Bible as *clear* and *practical* as possible. An observer who attended one of Moody's Sunday morning services described Moody's style in this way: "His sermon or lecture is little more than an exposition of a Bible truth, or a dramatic reading of a Bible story, with continuous application to his hearers."[14] Moody himself affirmed that his goals were to be as direct and relevant as possible—goals that sought the building up of his listeners, not himself:

∞

A good many preachers say I am lowering the pulpit. I am glad I am. I am trying to get it down to the level of men's hearts. If I wanted to hit Chicago I would not put the cannon on the top of this building and fire into the air. Too many preachers fire into the air.[15]

If God has given you a message, go and give it to the people as God has given it to you. It is a stupid thing to try to be eloquent.[16]

∞

115

Those who were critical or suspicious of Moody's extraordinary success often said he attracted huge crowds through his powerful charisma, his masterful understanding of human psychology, or through cleverness of some sort. But it was Moody's commitment to teaching God's Word alone that drew the hordes of genuinely interested listeners. He knew that the Bible alone had the power to speak to the deepest needs of the human heart and satisfy them. Commentators noted his success reflected this dependence on the Scriptures to move every man and woman.

> There are those who fancy that one must take up topics and truth outside the Bible, if he is to draw and hold the crowds. But who, in our day, has drawn and held such crowds to the very last as has Mr. Moody? And these crowds were composed of all classes; rich and poor, scholars, men of science, statesmen, noblemen, students, uneducated men and women, thieves, harlots, murderers, criminals of all sorts, absolutely all classes, and what had he to give them?—absolutely nothing but the Bible. Nothing else draws like that.[17]

> We see demonstrated in him not only the power of the Bible to draw men, but something higher far; the power of the Bible to save men. He not only drew vast audiences to hear, but . . . hundreds of thousands have gone away from hearing him saved. Saved by the power of this book. Some wise, advanced, philosophical, and

very self-sufficient preachers have laughed at Mr. Moody's narrowness and his mediaevalism; but let them point to results one hundredth part as beneficent as those that accompanied his "narrow and antiquated preaching."[18]

Many teachers in Moody's day felt the Bible itself was antiquated and no longer relevant to modern man. The school of higher criticism—which questioned much of the truthfulness of God's Word—had influenced many ministers to adopt a more philosophical and analytical approach to the Christian faith. Others felt the answers to man's problems lay in resolving social problems—hence, the social gospel. So widespread were the advocates of higher criticism and the social gospel that when Moody came on the scene, he stood out as refreshingly different. And there was power in his teaching because God's Word alone has the power to transform lives. God has promised us His Word will never return void (Isaiah 55:11); it will always draw a response. We don't need to help it along.

Moody's own response to those who didn't think the Bible was enough to meet the needs of people was this:

A great many people seem to think that the Bible is out of date, that it is an old book, that it has passed its day. They say it was very good for the dark ages, and that there is some very good history in it, but it was not intended for the present time; we are living

117

in a very enlightened age and men can get on very well without it; we have outgrown it.

Now, you might just as well say that the sun, which has shone so long, is now so old that it is out of date, and that whenever a man builds a house he need not put any windows in it, because we have a newer light and a better light; we have gaslight and electric light. These are something new; and I would advise people, if they think the Bible is too old and worn out, when they build houses, not to put windows in them, but just to light them with electric light; that is something new and that is what they are anxious for.[19]

And regarding the power and veracity of the Bible, in one of the final messages of his long life of ministry, Moody said,

I thank God for the old Book. I thank God for this old promise. It is as sweet and fresh today as it has ever been. Thank God, none of those promises are out of date, or grown stale. They are as fresh, and vigorous, and young, and sweet as ever.[20]

Believe in the Bible as God's revelation to you, and act accordingly. Do not reject any portion because it contains the supernatural or because you cannot understand it. Reverence all Scripture. Remember God's own estimate of it: "Thou has magnified thy word above all thy name."[21]

Even the fact that Moody didn't know how to answer some of the hard questions critics raise against the Bible didn't perturb him. He viewed the mysteries of God's Word as confirmation that the Bible was of divine origin, and not human.

I'm glad there are things in the Bible I don't understand. If I could take that book up and read it as I would any other book, I might think I could write a book like that, or that you could. I am glad there are heights I haven't been able to climb to. I am glad there are depths I haven't been able to fathom. It's the best proof that the book came from God.[22]

–A DEEP, UNSHAKEABLE LOVE–

Though Moody may have lacked a theological education, he did not lack at all when it came to one of the most important qualities of a spiritual leader: a deep and unshakeable love for God's Word. It was this love that generated his enthusiasm for its message and his passion for proclaiming it.

Dr. Charles Erdman summed all this up well in a tribute he gave at a Northfield conference some years after Moody's death:

> Mr. Moody did love the Bible. I suppose there is no other word I could properly use to express his affection, his devotion, his continual delight in this word of God. He liked to have even a certain copy of the Bible; he liked to have a good copy which he could mark, which he could fill with notes, which he could make a treasure-house of sermon outlines and illustrations, and all that was most precious to him. . . . You could not go into [his study] room for five minutes without realizing the man who studied in that room loved the Bible. That was the one book presented to you whichever way you turned.
>
> He taught people to love the Bible, and every man to have a good Bible. . . . Mr. Moody used to encourage people to carry their Bibles to church. He used to say that a man who walked a mile to church and carried his Bible preached a sermon a mile long. And I think he was right in this desire to have people come to individually possess a particular copy that they could learn to know and really to love. He was giving Bible readings,

Bible sermons, had Bible schools and Bible conferences, wherever he went. It was that book that was most precious to him of all books in the world.[23]

When your service to the Lord is all said and done, will those who are given the task of describing your ministry be able to say you were one who loved the Bible? Will they be able to say you were as a water well that overflowed constantly with clean and refreshing nourishment from the Word of Life?

MOODY
with His Pen

THE BIBLE for the last forty years has been the dearest thing on earth to me, and now I give a copy as my first gift to my first grandchild, Irene Moody, with a prayer that it may be her companion through life and guide her to those mansions that Christ has gone to prepare for those who love and serve Him on earth.

—D. L. Moody [24]

Inscription written by Moody in a Bible given to his first grandchild

CHAPTER SEVEN

A Faith
That Believes and
Trusts God

THE LORD IS MY ROCK AND MY FORTRESS AND MY DELIVERER; MY GOD, MY STRENGTH, IN WHOM I WILL TRUST.

—PSALM 18:2

When we have great faith, we can achieve great good.

That's the pattern we see all through the Bible. When Abraham failed to trust God, he lied to the Egyptians about Sarah. Compare that to the result when Abraham trusted God with his beloved son Isaac upon an altar.

When the nation of Israel failed to trust God and enter the Promised Land, the people were banished to the wilderness for forty years—and none of them ever did go into the land.

They all died in the wilderness, replaced by a new generation. Only Caleb and Joshua, who had faith in God's ability to defeat the powerful enemies that inhabited the land, were permitted to enter forty years later.

It was a lack of faith that made it possible for a nine-foot-tall giant to send an entire Israelite army cowering away in fear. It took one small and unprotected shepherd boy's faith to slay the huge soldier.

When Elijah trusted God, he won a most astounding and lopsided victory over four hundred prophets of Baal. But when one woman, Jezebel, made murderous threats, Elijah's faith had a meltdown of major proportions—and he fled far, far away.

When Peter trusted the Lord, he achieved a feat no man had ever done, nor has done since. He walked on water. But the very second he allowed doubt to creep into his mind, he sank. Fast.

In every case, faith was the ingredient that made the difference. Faith will carry us, and doubt will sink us.

−ENERGIZED WITH FAITH−

It was faith that energized Dwight L. Moody to achieve great good for God's kingdom. Every endeavor began with faith and prayer—his schools, his evangelistic campaigns, his church ministries, his conferences for equipping ministry workers, his publishing endeavors, his outreach to prison inmates, and more.

What's particularly notable about Moody's faith is that it was a continuously abiding and ongoing expression of trust in God. In other words, he didn't just try to summon up faith at the moments he needed it. He lived in a perpetual awareness that God is always at work, opening some doors and closing others. Moody's desire was to walk in step with wherever the Lord might take him, with a faith always ready to act. This is demonstrated well in the story about how Moody happened to acquire the land to begin his first school, Northfield Seminary. Biographer Lyle Dorsett provides an excellent account of what took place that momentous day in 1878:

> While the Northfield Seminary was still in its planning stages, Marshall [a merchant from Boston] and Moody were walking Moody's land and looking for the best site for building a classroom facility. In what Moody quick-ly concluded was an obvious act of God and, therefore, a clear sign that the seminary vision should go forward in all haste, he and Marshall cast their eyes on some sandy, hilly land adjacent to Moody's property. It was barren soil, seemingly unfit for cultivation and even worthless for pasture. Just as they were surveying this bleak hill with apparently little going for it except a spectacular view of the Connecticut River, the owner rode up. Moody inquired how much land he owned

there; the neighbor guessed about sixteen acres. Marshall and Moody immediately asked him if he would sell. Having no use for the property himself, he signed it away that day for a reasonable price.[1]

Moody, then, was marked by a constant watchfulness for opportunities and a readiness to exercise faith that God would bring about whatever results He desired.

–A DEFINITION OF FAITH–

Simply put, faith is *trusting God*. In every one of the biblical examples mentioned at the beginning of this chapter—Abraham, the nation of Israel and Caleb and Joshua, David, Elijah, Peter—the difference between failure and success was a complete trust that rested in God. In one of his messages, Moody defined faith this way:

∞

The best definition I can find of faith is the dependence upon the veracity of another. The Bible definition in the 11th chapter of Hebrews is, "Faith is the substance of things hoped for, the evidence of things not seen." In other words, faith says amen to everything that God says. Faith takes God without any ifs. If God says it, Faith says I believe it; Faith says amen to it.[2]

∞

Later in that same sermon, he said,

∞

If God tells us to do a thing we are to do it; if He tells us to believe a thing, we are to believe it; we are to have faith in God. Have faith in God, and if God tells you to believe a thing believe it, and then you will have peace and confidence and joy.[3]

∞

Moody also pointed out that when it comes to faith, it's a matter of placing all our confidence in God and none in ourselves:

∞

Your strength lies in God, and not in yourself. The moment you lean on yourself, down you go. The moment we get self-contented and think we are able to stand and overcome, we are on dangerous territory; we are standing upon the edge of a precipice. When I first became a Christian I thought I would be glad when I got farther on, and got established. I thought I would be so strong and there would not be any danger; but the longer I live, the more danger I see there is. The only hope of any Christian . . . is to keep hold of Christ.[4]

Faith is an outward look, not an inward look.[5]

∞

−THE OBJECT OF OUR FAITH:
OUR GREAT GOD−

How often can we trust God? That question may seem to have an overly obvious answer—we can *always* trust Him. At least, that's what we say. Yet each time we allow worry, anxiety, or fear to gnaw at our minds and hearts is a time we've failed to trust the Lord and exercise faith in Him. Because the responsibilities and burdens of spiritual leadership are so many and often difficult, we who are in positions of leadership are vulnerable, on many fronts, to situations or circumstances that will assail our faith.

At the times we find it hard to express faith, it's helpful to consider who God is and what He can do. For example,

- He's *omnipotent* . . . which means He's all-powerful and nothing can overrule His will.

- He's *omniscient* . . . which means He's all-knowing, so nothing ever takes Him by surprise, and He knows exactly what will happen in our future.

- He's *omnipresent* . . . which means He's everywhere and is always with us.

- He is *all-sufficient* . . . which means He can provide for our every spiritual and physical need.

So no matter how great the problem before us, God is greater. No matter how intimidating the circumstance we're in, God is greater. No matter what size the obstacle that looms over us, God is greater.

Moody affirmed these truths when he said:

∞

The way to get faith is to know who God is, and I never knew a man or woman that was well acquainted with God that wanted faith. Some one said to a Scotch woman, "You are a woman of great faith." "No," she says, "I am a woman of little faith, but I have got a great God." [6]

There is nothing in heaven, earth, or hell too hard for our God, and it is a good thing for us to start out with this thought that God is able to do above all that we dare think or ask. [7]

A great many things may seem very hard for us; but let us bear in mind that nothing is too hard for God. "Oh, Lord God! Behold thou has made the heaven and the earth by thy great power and stretched-out arm." . . . Think how God created this world; think of its mighty rivers and mighty mountains, and its depths and its plains; and yet some one has said it is only a little ball thrown from the hand of the Almighty. They tell us that the sun is thirteen hundred thousand times larger than this world. . . . And we are told that light travels at one hundred and eighty six thousand miles a [second]. . . . Now, if this is true, think of our great and our mighty God![8]

∞

As Moody said, ultimately, it all comes down to remembering one little word:

∞

That little word "able"—may it sink down deep into your hearts. . . . He is able to do all for you that you need to have done; and if you but make up your minds to rely on Him you will have strength as you need it.[9]

∞

–When We Feel Discouraged–

Because we who are spiritual leaders are on the front lines of advancing God's kingdom, we are frequently in the hottest parts of the battle. As Moody said,

∞

The fiercest attacks are made on the strongest forts, and the fiercer the battle the young believer is called on to wage, the surer evidence it is of the work of the

Holy Spirit in his heart. God will not desert him in his time of need, any more than He deserted His people of old when they were hard pressed by their foes.[10]

∞

Given the likelihood for attack—whether through temptation, through our own fleshly desires, or through Satan's attempts to derail us—we can expect we'll have times when fears and worries do get a foothold in our lives. We can expect that for as long as God is at work within us building our faith, we will face increasingly difficult circumstances that call for us to exercise even greater faith in Him. But sometimes our response isn't one of faith. Sometimes we allow seeds of doubt to germinate in the soil of our thoughts and grow—to the point that we become discouraged or even depressed.

Moody describes one such trial he faced:

∞

I remember years ago I got discouraged because I could not see much fruit from my work. One morning, when I was in my study, much depressed, one of my Sunday-school teachers came in and wanted to know what I was discouraged about, and I told him it was because I could see no results from my work. "By the way," he said, "did you ever study the character of Noah?" I thought I knew all about Noah, and I told him so; but he said, "Now, if you have never studied Noah carefully, you ought to do it, for I cannot tell you what a blessing his example has been for me." After he went out I took my Bible and commenced to read about Noah, and the thought came stealing over me, "Here is a man who toiled and worked a hundred years and didn't get discouraged; if he did, the Holy Ghost didn't put it on record." The clouds lifted, and I got up and said, "If the Lord wants me to work without any fruit I will work on."

That day I went down to the noon prayer-meeting, and when I saw the people coming to pray I said to myself, "Noah worked a hundred years, and he never saw a prayer-meeting outside of his own family." Pretty soon a man got up, right across the aisle from where I was sitting, and said he had come from a little town where a hundred had united with the church the year before. And I thought to myself, "What if Noah had heard that! He preached so many, many years and didn't get a convert, yet he was not discouraged." I made up my mind then, that, God helping me, I would never get discouraged again. I would do the best I could, and leave the results with God, and it has been a wonderful help to me.[11]

∞

Moody's discouragement stemmed from the fact he wasn't seeing results in his ministry. He came to realize that though he didn't seem to be bearing fruit, that was no reason for him to stop serving and cease trusting God. We're called merely to be faithful, and as Moody said, "leave the results with God."

This raises an important point: While great faith enables us to do great good, we should be cautious about what we perceive to be great results, because God's perspective of great results is likely to be different from ours. In His eyes, even "small" results can be great—such as the return of the one lost sheep in Luke 15:4–7. So while we would do well to emulate Moody's trust in God, we should never compare our results to his. God has given each one of us a unique purpose, a unique place of ministry. Ours may be a very small stewardship, numbering only a few people. To God, it's not the size of our ministry that matters, but that we are placing complete trust in Him as we carry on that ministry.

How did Moody get over his discouragement? Note that he took his eyes off his circumstances and placed them on the Lord. While he didn't necessarily have an answer or a remedy to the situation itself, he did know whom to turn to. That's why he could give this advice:

∞

My friends, if you go to the Lord with your troubles
He will take them away. Would you not rather be

with the Lord and get rid of your troubles, than be with your troubles and without God? Let trouble come, if it will drive us nearer to God.[12]

For twenty years I have made this a rule. Christ is just as habitually near, as personally present to me as any other person living; and when I have any troubles, trials, and afflictions, I go to Him with them. When I want counsel I go to Him, just as if I could talk face to face with Him.[13]

Caleb and Joshua are great favorites of mine. They have got a ring about them. They were not all the time looking at the hindrances and obstacles in their way; they got their eyes above them.[14]

There is one passage of Scripture which has always been a great comfort to me. In the eighth chapter of Romans Paul says, "All things work together for good to them that love God [KJV]". Some years ago a child of mine had scarlet fever. I went to the druggist's [office] to get the medicine which the doctor had ordered, and told him to be sure and be very careful in making up the prescription. The druggist took down one bottle after another, in any one of which there might be what would be rank poison for my child; but he stirred them together and mixed *them up, and made just the medicine which my child needed. And so God gives us a little adversity here, a little prosperity there, and all works for our good.*[15]

∞

In line with Scripture's exhortation for us to cast all our cares upon the Lord (1 Peter 5:7), Moody said,

∞

A minister was one day moving his library upstairs. As he was going up with a load of books, his little boy came in, and was very anxious to help his father. So his father just told him to go and get an armful, and bring them upstairs. When the father came back, he met the little fellow about half-way up, tugging away at the biggest book in the library. He couldn't manage to carry it up. It was too big. So he sat down and cried.

His father found him, and just took him in his arms, book and all, and carried him upstairs. So Christ will carry you and all your burdens, if you will but let Him.[16]

∞

Also, in times when we find it hard to trust God, we can take comfort in knowing that our afflictions here on earth are temporary. They will last for but a moment compared to the perfect bliss and glory that is ours for all eternity:

∞

Yes, there is a glorious day before us in the future. . . . That's what kept Paul rejoicing. He said, "These light afflictions, these few stripes, these few brickbats and stones that they throw at me—why, the glory that is beyond excels them so much that I count them as nothing, nothing at all, so that I may win Christ."

And so, when things go against us, let us cheer up; let us remember that the night will soon pass away and the morning dawn upon us. . . . Glorious future, my friends! Yes, glorious day! And it may be a great deal nearer than many of us think. During these few days we are here let us stand steadfast and firm, and by and by we shall be in the unbroken circle in yon world of light, and have the King in our midst.[17]

∞

–Persevering in Faith–

It's never difficult for us to express our faith in the Lord when life is going well. It's only when the going gets rough and there's seemingly no end to it that we find it hard to trust God.

And that's when we need to anchor ourselves to the Lord's promises to care for us and carry us through. We can look to Him to enable us to be courageous and persevere:

∞

We must fight with the courage of a Joshua. I have learned one thing since I went into the school of Christ, and that is, that God never takes a man for His purposes who is weak; he must have confidence in himself through Christ; must not hang on his own strength, but must have courage, and must believe that God is willing and ready to aid him.[18]

Those who have been greatly used of God in all ages have been men of courage. If we are full of faith we shall not be full of fear, distrusting God all the while. That is the trouble with the Church of Christ today—there are so many who are fearful, because they do not believe that God is going to use them. What we need is to have the courage that will compel us to move forward.[19]

Another thing we need is what Spurgeon used to call stick-to-it-iveness. One of our failings is that we don't persevere. We are good in spots. We are good a few days or a few months in the year. We work pretty well spasmodically, but it is the long and steady pull that does the work, and we want men that are not simply passing through occasional revivals, but who are in revival state all the time.[20]

∞

Before Joshua led the nation of Israel into the Promised Land and against the indomitable fortress-city of Jericho, God told him, "Be strong and of good courage; do not be afraid, nor be dismayed, for the Lord your God is with you wherever you go" (Joshua 1:9). As we know, Joshua didn't allow seemingly impossible circumstances to sway his faith. He simply moved forward and did what God told him to do . . . and knew the Lord would take care of the rest.

That principle is applicable to every area of our leadership. No matter how great the problem, God is greater. We may experience trials for the moment, and the Lord doesn't expect us to resolve them on our own. Rather, He calls us to trust Him. And to persevere. When we do so, we allow Him to accomplish whatever it is He wants to achieve through our lives. And through it all, we'll grow into stronger spiritual leaders. As Moody said,

∞

Dear friends, let us expect that God is going to use us. Let us have courage and go forward, looking to God to do great things.[21]

∞

MOODY
on His Knees

OUR HEAVENLY FATHER, may we look for a blessing ere we go hence, for precious blessings before we go out of this place. We would ask Thee to bless every minister. . . . Next Sunday may they enter their pulpits weaker than they have ever been before. May they lose all their own strength and receive from Thee that which is so necessary to the work. . . . Increase our faith; take away our miserable unbelief. . . . May all these men receive from on high the power they need so much.[22]

^A Fervent
Commitment
To Holiness

PRESENT YOUR BODIES A LIVING
SACRIFICE, HOLY, ACCEPTABLE
TO GOD, WHICH IS YOUR
REASONABLE SERVICE.

ROMANS 12:1

"I have no desire to make an impact on the world for God."

Imagine a spiritual leader making that declaration. How would you react if you heard that from a spiritual leader? Such a statement would seem rather odd, wouldn't it? After all, to *not* want to make an impact runs completely contrary to the main goals of spiritual leadership: (1) pointing non-Christians toward salvation and (2) urging Christians toward spiritual growth. Both require having an impact.

Good spiritual leadership and having an impact are inseparable. To illustrate this, here's an experiment you can try. Get a sheet of paper, and write your ministry job description. You might be the senior pastor of a megachurch, or a mentor for just one other believer. You might be the administrator of a large Christian school, or a parent who cares enough to lead his or her children by example. Perhaps you're the director of all the Sunday school classes in your church, or an assistant helper in the preschool class. Whatever the case, after you've written your job description, ask yourself: Does this position call for me to make an impact on other lives?

No matter what your role, the answer will be yes. The job of every spiritual leader—no matter how big or small—is to influence others forward and upward in Christ.

It's probably safe to say that deep down in our hearts, all of us who have been entrusted with any level of spiritual leadership want to have an impact on our sphere of influence. We want to contribute to bringing change in people's lives. We want to be thought of as someone who is making a difference. And we may even have hopes that by the time we die, we will have left some sort of lasting legacy that will continue the work of extending the Lord's kingdom.

–HOW TO HAVE IMPACT–

So what is it that enables us to have impact?

If you've read anything about spiritual leadership, chances are you've come across all kinds of ideas and suggestions for having a greater influence on others. Some are of value, and some aren't. But virtually all of those guidelines are insignificant compared to the one thing that really does create an impact—the one quality that really does give us influence.

Holiness.

People Will Notice It

A holy life grabs people's attention. Both believers and unbelievers cannot help but notice it. D. L. Moody was right when he said, "A holy life will produce the deepest impression. Lighthouses blow no horns; they only shine."[1] A holy life is like a piercing light that shines brilliantly to those on the dark and stormy seas of life. But when there's no light, there's no reference point. The unlit lighthouse blends into the darkness and the mist—rendering it useless and without impact.

That's why Jesus said, "Let your light so shine before men, that they may see your good works and glorify your Father in heaven" (Matthew 5:16). That's why Paul commanded that we "become blameless and harmless, children of God without fault in the midst of a crooked and perverse generation, among whom you shine as lights in the world" (Philippians 2:15).

Sin Will Block It

In both passages, light is equated with making an impact. A holy life is a life that allows Christ's light to shine unobscured, showing people the way they ought to go. But when we allow sin a place in our hearts, we eclipse our Lord's light. We end up blocking the impact He can have through us—rendering ourselves useless. In essence, we become as one who says, "I have no desire to make an impact on the world for God."

Moody put it this way:

∞

God has sent us into the world to shine for Him—to light up this dark world. Christ came to be the Light of the World, but men put out that light. They took it to Calvary and blew it out. Before Christ went up on high, He said to His disciples, "You are the light of the world. You are My witnesses. Go forth and carry the gospel to the perishing nations of the earth." [2]

A man may preach with the eloquence of an angel, but if he doesn't live what he preaches, and act out in his home and his business what he professes, his testimony goes for naught, and the people say it is all hypocrisy after all; it is all a sham. Words are very empty, if there is nothing back of them. Your testimony is poor and worthless, if there is not a record back of that testimony consistent with what you profess. What we need is to pray to God to lift us up out of this low, cold, formal state that we live in, that we may dwell in the atmosphere of God continually, and that the Lord may lift upon us the light of His countenance, and that we may shine in this world, reflecting His grace and glory.[3]

Moody was also careful to stress that we are not the source of this light, but God: "Then we must remember that we are to *let* our light shine. It does not say, '*Make* your light shine.' You do not have to *make* light to shine; all you have to do is to *let* it shine."[4]

–A Watching World–

Children, for the most part, are like their parents. Observe a child for a little while, and you can start guessing what his or her parents are like. Similarly, the way you speak and act as a child of God will lead other people to certain conclusions about your heavenly Father. Are they getting an accurate picture of Him?

That's a sobering question to ask, but ask it we must. As spiritual leaders, we have many eyes on us. There's a lot at stake—

no less than the reputations of God Himself and the Christian faith. That's why holiness is so important. At a conference for Christian leaders and workers, Moody said,

∽

The eyes of the world are upon us. They don't read the Bible, but they read you and me, and we talk more by our walk than in any other way. We are "living epistles, known and read of all men." . . . I said to some one the other day, "That man must have been in the army or in a military school." He said, "Yes; how did you know?" I said, "By the way he walks." There are some people that you can tell have been with Jesus Christ by their walk.[5]

Many a person who is engaged in active Christian work, or who takes a leading part in the prayer meeting, is so faulty in his daily walk as to be a stumbling-block to others. Sometimes the last people to be favorably impressed by professing Christians are those who know them in their home life. This is all wrong. Test yourselves therefore and see if you indulge in any questionable habit, anything in your example and influence that is likely to lead astray those who read your conduct.[6]

And in his book *The Faith Which Overcomes*, he said,

Where one man reads the Bible, a hundred read you and me. That is what Paul meant when he said we were to be living epistles, known and read of all men. . . . If we do not commend the Gospel to people by our holy walk and conversation, we shall not win them to Christ. Some little act of kindness will perhaps do more to influence them than any number of long sermons.[7]

We might be tempted to respond, "Well, compared to other leaders, my realm of influence is small. If something is wrong in my life, it might be noticed by a very few . . . if at all. Surely this is not as much a concern for me as it is for those who are more prominent or have more significant roles in the Lord's work." But as Moody wisely pointed out,

What God wants you to do is to use the influence you have. Daniel probably did not have much influence down in Babylon at first, but God soon gave him more because he was faithful and used what he had.[8]

When you make good use of your opportunities to have a little influence, God will then know He can trust you with greater influence.

–When God Uses Us–

A Clear and Useful Channel

On farms that use irrigation ditches, one never-ending chore is to make sure that debris has not fallen into the ditches, thereby blocking the life-nourishing water from getting to the plants. Similarly, we who are spiritual leaders need to examine our hearts for any debris that would restrict God's ability to work through us. A holy life is a useful life.

∞

There is one requisite for being used of God which must be emphasized. You will remember how Paul, in writing to Timothy on this subject, says: "Let every one that nameth the name of Christ depart from iniquity." It will be the height of madness for you to attempt to work for God if there is any iniquity in your heart that you are unwilling to part with.[9]

Now let me say no man or woman is fit to work for God until they become peculiar in this Bible sense—until they give up sinful, worldly pleasures, and separate themselves to live and work for God.

Then see how God will bless them. God grant that all may become chosen vessels and meet for the Master's use.[10]

Apart from the World

Presenting ourselves to God as clean and useful vessels requires ongoing discernment on our part. It requires that we "test all things; hold fast what is good. Abstain from every form of evil" (1 Thessalonians 5:21–22). It requires that we "not present [our] members as instruments of unrighteousness to sin, but present [ourselves] to God . . . and [our] members as instruments of righteousness to God" (Romans 6:13).

It's especially helpful to remember why Christ came to earth to die on the cross. He "gave Himself for us, that He might redeem us from every lawless deed and purify for Himself His own special people, zealous for good works" (Titus 2:14). He gave Himself up for the church "that He might sanctify and cleanse her with the washing of water by the word, that He might present her to Himself a glorious church, not having spot or wrinkle or any such thing, but that she should be holy and without blemish" (Ephesians 5:26–27).

With those truths in mind, these exhortations from Moody take on greater significance:

∞

Consecration means separation. If you want power, you can have it, but it may mean that you must give up a great many things. Any one can go with the world, but it takes strong character to go against the current.[11]

Jesus taught His disciples that they must be in the world but not of it. A Christian in the world is one thing, and the world in a Christian is quite another thing. A ship in the water is all right, but when the water gets into the ship, it is quite a different thing. The churches are full of men and women who have no power at all. Where did they lose it? It was when they formed an alliance with the world.[12]

∞

That raises an important question: What exactly is "the world"? From what are we to separate ourselves? Moody gave this answer . . . and particularly noteworthy is what he said about Christians who try to walk as closely to the world as they can without becoming part of it:

∞

Anything that interrupts our communion with God—that hinders the progress of the spiritual life, and that chills our affection for Christ. Anything that does that, we ought to give up. If we are willing to do so, Christ will more than make it up to us. Many Christians seem to have the desire to live as near the world as they possibly can—to have as much of the world as they can, and have Christ at the same time. My experience has been that such Christians are the most wretched people on the face of the earth. They neither enjoy the world nor Christ. They are what are called border Christians, running a little over the line, mingling with the world today, and coming back among Christ's people tomorrow. [13]

Being Free from Sin's Snare

Anytime Moody spoke to groups of Christian workers, one of his prevailing themes was a life set apart for God and free from entanglement with sin. He urged his fellow servants to guard their minds and hearts against even seemingly "trivial" sins— warning that even one small vice, left unchecked, can quickly overtake us.

Is there some habit marring your Christian life, hindering your usefulness, checking your progress in divine life? Then make up your mind that you are going to get victory over it. It may look like a small enemy, but it will become stronger and stronger if not checked.

151

Sin multiplies. The tendency to sin gathers force with every new commission. . . . We must either overcome sin or it will overcome us; we must take our choice. Have you completely forsaken your sins, or is there some enemy you allow to remain alive?[14]

When I was speaking to five thousand children in Glasgow some years ago, I took a spool of thread and said to one of the largest boys:

"Do you believe I can bind you with that thread?"

He laughed at the idea. I wound the thread around him a few times, and he broke it with a single jerk. Then I wound the thread around and around, and by and by I said:

"Now get free if you can."

He couldn't move head or foot. If you are slave to some vile habit, you must either slay that habit, or it will slay you.[15]

–A RIGHT STANDING WITH GOD–

In the life of a spiritual leader, sin's influence can have a ripple effect that extends outward to other lives. It's much like the way an oil spill can seep outward from a cracked ship hull and bring deadly harm to all the innocents in its wake. It is because of sin's frequently subtle but devastating effects that Moody gives us this wise counsel:

Keep short accounts with God. You should see the face of God every morning before you see the face of any human being. If you come to the cross every morning, you never will get but one day's journey from the cross. . . . Just keep close to the cross, and close to Him, and if anything has gone wrong during the day or evening, do not sleep until that account has been settled. Take it to Christ and tell it right out to Him; tell Him how you are sorry, and ask Him to forgive you. He delights to forgive.[16]

There is nothing the world so wants as holy men. The cause of Christ is paralyzed because of sin—sin in believers. . . . It may be some hidden sin that keeps God from using us more. Let us be honest with God, and ask Him to search us and show us ourselves. Let David's prayer be ours: "Search me, O my God"—not my neighbors, nor other people, but "Search me!"[17]

Are our hearts clean in God's sight? Or are we clinging to a small pleasure or two we find too hard to give up? No matter how much we might rationalize that one little sin hidden deep within us surely won't affect our ministry, the simple fact is, it will. As Galatians 5:16 says, it's impossible to walk in the Spirit and fulfill the lust of the flesh at the same time. Either we're filled with the Spirit or we're not. Either we're yielding our bodies as instruments of righteousness or we're not. Either we're living in obedience or we're not.

There's nothing more refreshing, more liberating, more fulfilling than letting go of all sin in our lives. When we have a clear conscience, we can stand before God with full confidence and joy. But when we entertain sin—no matter how small—we can no longer look God straight in the eyes. And we become prisoners to fear because we're afraid that our wrong might be discovered by others.

–An Ongoing Battle–

Can we ever get to the point in our spiritual growth where sin and temptation become less and less of a problem to us? At first, Moody thought the answer was yes, but then discovered he was wrong—for the more God uses us, the more Satan becomes anxious to defeat us.

When I was converted I made this mistake: I thought the battle was already mine, the victory already won, the crown already in my grasp. I thought that old things had passed away, that all things had become new; that my old corrupt nature, the Adam life, was gone. But I found out, after serving Christ for a few months, that conversion was only like enlisting in the army; that there was a battle on hand, and that if I was to get a crown, I had to work for it and fight for it.[18]

There was a time when I was first converted when I used to think that when I got to be a Christian of twenty years standing I should rejoice, because there would be no danger of my falling then. My friends, there is more danger now than there was then. Do you know why? Because the more useful a man becomes the better target he is for the devil.[19]

∞

–THE PROMISE OF VICTORY–

Though we know temptation and sin will haunt us for the rest of our lives here on earth, we can rest in knowing our heavenly Father hasn't left us without the resources we need for victory.

∞

I have either got to overcome the world, or the world is going to overcome me. I have either got to conquer sin in me—or sin about me—and get it under my feet, or it is going to conquer me. . . . We have this to encourage us: we are assured of victory at the end. We are promised a glorious triumph.[20]

When He said on the cross, "It is finished!" it was the shout of a conqueror. He had overcome every enemy. He had met sin and death. He had met every foe that you and I have got to meet, and had come off victor. Now if I have got the Spirit of Christ, if I have got that same life in me, then it is that I have got a power that is greater than any power in the world; and with that same power I overcome the world.[21]

∞

Because Christ and the Spirit dwell in us, we have within us a power greater than any temptation or sin that might arise. We *can* say no to temptation; we *can* resist sin. We *can* "lay aside every weight, and the sin which so easily ensnares us, and . . . run with endurance the race that is set before us, looking unto Jesus, the author and finisher of our faith" (Hebrews 12:1–2).

MOODY
from the Pulpit

Scripture commands us to live holy because God is holy. "As He who called you is holy, you also be holy in all your conduct, because it is written, 'Be holy, for I am holy'" (1 Peter 1:15–16). As His children, we're to reflect His likeness to those around us. When we reflect Him poorly, people will see a poor image of Him. And when we reflect Him clearly, people will see a clear image of Him.

It is well said that ministry is a character profession. May personal holiness, then, be our personal passion—so that we might have a real and lasting impact as spiritual leaders.

CHAPTER NINE

^A Heart
Marked by
Humility

WALK WORTHY OF THE CALLING
WITH WHICH YOU WERE
CALLED, WITH ALL LOWLINESS
AND GENTLENESS.

—EPHESIANS 4:1–2

Late one night while walking through the halls of one of the campus buildings at Northfield, D. L. Moody noticed a pair of boots outside one of the doors. To most people the significance of this would have been lost, but because Moody had traveled to Europe, he knew of the European custom of leaving shoes outside one's hotel door to be shined. The owner of the shoes, however, didn't realize this wasn't done in America. Because Moody was aware this might happen, he had earlier instructed a student—the assigned doorman for the evening—and said, "If our guest from Paris places his shoes outside his door, make sure they are shined by morning."

The student's reply suggested a reluctance to do the task, but Moody left the matter at that, allowing the student a chance to change his mind and do the job. Early the next morning, Moody arose and discovered the shoes had not yet been shined. So he picked them up, took them downstairs, blackened them, and brought them back.[1]

This quiet act of lowly service was very typical of Moody. In the years following his death, numerous people shared similar stories of small and secret kindnesses one would not expect from a minister of Moody's stature. These accounts reveal a genuinely humble leader with a benevolent heart—one who had learned well the example set by the Lord Jesus when He took upon Himself a task normally reserved for the lowest of servants or slaves and washed the feet of His disciples.

F. B. Meyer, a well-known minister and author from England who was a frequent speaker at Moody's Northfield conferences, gave this tribute of Moody:

> He was absolutely simple and humble. In all the numberless hours I have spent with him he never once manifested the least sign of affectation, never drew attention to himself, never alluded to the vast numbers that had attended his meetings, the distinguished

persons who had confided their secrets to him, or the enterprises which had originated in his suggestion or been cradled under his care.[2]

−"He Put Himself in the Background"−

In fact, because Meyer was often at Northfield, he would have nodded in agreement upon hearing this assessment of Moody from R. A. Torrey:

> He constantly put himself in the background, and put others forward. So it was to the end. He refused again and again to speak at Northfield, because he wished to sit as a learner at the feet of two young men thirty-three years old. He was constantly expecting to learn from other people.
>
> How many men whom God has led out and greatly used in America have become puffed up, and God has had to lay them aside; but Mr. Moody was never laid aside. God used him to the end.[3]

There's also a rather humorous anecdote Moody liked to share with his friends that is yet another indicator of his humility. With very little time to escape their house during the Chicago Fire of 1871, Mrs. Moody was determined to rescue a portrait in oil of her husband, which hung on the wall of their parlor. Mrs. Moody urged Dwight to save the painting. His reaction?

"Take my own picture!" he said. "Well, that would be amusing! Suppose I am met on the street by friends in the same plight as ourselves, and they say: 'Hello, Moody, glad you escaped; what's that you have saved and cling to so affectionately?'—wouldn't it sound well to reply, 'Oh, I've got my own portrait'?"

No entreaty could prevail on Mr. Moody, but the canvas was hastily knocked out of the heavy frame, and carried off by Mrs. Moody herself—the one relic rescued from their home.[4]

A copy of that portrait, perhaps the most well-known image of the evangelist, today hangs at the Moody Bible Institute—thanks to his wife's insistence.

–HUMILITY IS . . .–

In the Bible, one of the best—if not *the* best—definitions of humility is found in Philippians 2. At the beginning of the chapter, the apostle Paul wrote, "Let nothing be done through selfish ambition or conceit, but in lowliness of mind let each esteem others better than himself" (verse 3). To be of lowly mind is to not think highly of one's self, but to place one's self below others and put others first. And to esteem others better is to lift them up and seek their good before your own. Humility is about setting ourselves aside and putting others first.

But that's not all. Paul then presented the supreme example of humility: Jesus Christ. It was Christ who "made Himself of no reputation, taking the form of a bondservant, and coming in the likeness of men," and "humbled Himself and became obedient to the point of death, even the death of the cross" (verses 7–8). Christ, in His humility, went so far as to die for others. This is the highest possible form of self-sacrifice. What makes His example particularly remarkable is that He is the King of Kings and Lord of Lords. He who is worthy of the highest honors condescended Himself to the lowest of servants. If He, as the ultimate spiritual leader over all the world, was willing to humble Himself in such a fashion, how much more should we as mere human spiritual leaders be willing to do the same! Humility, then, is a complete setting aside of self for the benefit of others. It's none of self, and all of others.

Among the ways Moody defined and illustrated humility are these:

∞

[Humility] consists not in thinking meanly of ourselves, but in not thinking of ourselves at all. . . . If humility speaks of itself, it is gone.[5]

Some years ago I saw what is called a sensitive plant. I happened to breathe on it and suddenly it drooped its head; I touched it and it withered away.

Humility is as sensitive as that; it cannot safely be brought out on exhibition.[6]

∽

Moody also observed, "There is no harder lesson for man to learn than the lesson of humility. It is the rarest of all the gifts. It is a very rare thing to find a man or woman that is following closely the footsteps of the Master in meekness and humility."[7]

—EXHORTATIONS TO HUMILITY—

To the world, it's contradictory for a leader to exhibit humility. After all, it's expected that leaders seek prominence and power. They're expected to do whatever is necessary to climb to the top of the ladder. For the simple reason that we who were born in sin are naturally selfish, humility doesn't come easily.

God's standard, as we know, is the exact opposite of the world's. First Peter 5:5 tells us that "God resists the proud, but gives grace to the humble." James 4:10 says, "Humble yourselves in the sight of the Lord, and He will lift you up." Romans 12:10 says we're to "[give] preference to one another." And the greatest leader to ever walk on this earth, the Lord Jesus, said, "The Son of Man did not come to be served, but to serve" (Mark 10:45). That Christ did this successfully proves that it's not paradoxical at all to be a strong leader and, at the same time, practice humility in its highest form—complete self-sacrifice. Again, humility is none of self, and all of others.

Reflecting these spiritual truths, Moody taught several principles about humility; they reverberate through the corridors of time to us today. Consider these four principles found in Moody's sermons:

1. God Uses the Humble

∞

The first step to a higher service is the end of self. God's way up is down. God never yet lifted up a man high that He did not cast him down first; never. Self must be annihilated.[8]

God uses the foolish things, the weak things, the base things, the despised things, the things that are not. What for? That no flesh may glory in His sight.[9]

Very often when we are cast down, and are in our lowest position in the sight of the world, God lifts us to the very heights of glory.[10]

∞

2. Pride Hinders God's Work

∞

This eternal spirit of seeking to be great is one of the greatest obstacles today in the church of God. Oh, may God take it from our hearts, and may we have the spirit of the Master; may we know what it is to have the same mind that was in Christ, and he that will be great let him be the least of all. And when we have got at the end of this self-seeking, and are nothing in the sight of God, then we are fit channels for God to speak through.[11]

The great trouble with many is that we don't get our selves out of sight. We ought to let the name of Christ be kept in sight, and ever watch for Him, and then we are ready to work for the Lord in any position.[12]

There is one thing the Lord cannot have, and that is His disciples boasting in their strength. When a man thinks he has got a good deal of strength, and is self-confident, you may look for his downfall. It may be years before it comes to light, but it is already commenced. Peter did not fall all at once, but it was gradual and sure. The thing to do is to stand, and take heed lest ye fall. Beware! We have got terrible enemies, and we are very weak in ourselves.[13]

3. Our Strength Comes from God Alone

∞

All strength is borrowed strength. We get it from Christ.[14]

When we get to the end of our own power, then it is that the power of God is manifested in us.[15]

My dear friends, do you know that if we are linked to God and will let God work in us and use us, every one of us can do His work if we will, and the weaker, the stronger. It is the weakest that are the strongest after all. Those who are strong, who are going to do it in their own strength, make an utter failure. But when we haven't any strength of our own, then it is that we lay hold of God's strength, and then it is the work is done.[16]

∞

4. God Blesses the Humble

∞

He always blesses the humble, and, if we can get down in the dust before Him, no one will go away disappointed.[17]

∞

Several of these excerpts came from messages Moody gave to pastors and others involved in ministry service. Evidently he saw a need to urge other leaders to develop the virtue of humility. And Moody did not hold himself up as better than anyone else in this regard; he admitted to his need in this area as well. On one occasion he told some fellow leaders, "I have been studying the life of John the Baptist—and I have been ashamed of myself. If you have any regard for me, pray that I might have humility. When I put my life beside the life of some of these men I say, Shame on the Christianity of the present day." [18]

—HUMILITY AND ADMITTING WRONG—

Perhaps the most difficult form of humility is a willingness to approach someone we've wronged and ask for forgiveness. When those of us who "are supposed to know better" do something we know we shouldn't do, we find it hard to admit our error to others because it forces us to swallow our pride (which is exactly what God wants us to do!). This happens often in parent-child relationships and leader-follower relationships. It's painful to confess wrong to a subordinate because we then make ourselves vulnerable to the charge that we didn't live up to all that's expected of us, given our position of leadership and our supposed wisdom. But that's a risk we have to take, because ultimately, as Christians, we're called to be reconciled to our brother before we bring our gifts to God (Matthew 5:23–24). If we don't have a right relationship with another person, then we won't have a right relationship with God.

Moody himself took this risk and humbled himself, asking for forgiveness when he realized he had done wrong against someone. His son Will recalled one instance:

> One evening before an evangelistic meeting, a detractor approached Moody and insulted him. Moody's old temper broke out, and he thrust the man away, sending him reeling down some steps. The man left uninjured, but the altercation was witnessed by many onlookers. . . . Before Moody began the . . . meeting that night he arose, and with trembling voice made a humble apology.
>
> "Friends," he said, "before beginning tonight I want to confess that I yielded just now to my temper, out in the hall, and have done wrong. Just as I was coming in here tonight I lost my temper with a man, and I want to confess my wrong before you all, and if that man is present here whom I thrust away from me in anger I want to ask his forgiveness and God's. Let us pray." There was not a word of excuse or vindication for resenting the insult. The impression made by his words was wonderful, and instead of the meeting being killed by the scene it was greatly blessed by such a consistent and straightforward confession.[19]

On another occasion, when Moody became aware that he had deeply hurt a fellow worker in ministry, he wrote a letter of profuse apology:

∞

My dear Miss Anderson:

I cannot tell you how bad it makes me feel to think I hurt your feelings. I can see, though, I gave you good reason to feel hurt, but I did not intend to injure your feelings, and I hope you will forgive me, for I am sure I would not like to be guilty of offending you. There is scarcely one in the church that I think more of and pray more for than yourself, and I would rather give up my right hand than to do anything that would hinder you in your heavenly race. I love you as a teacher and as a member of the same fold and church that I am, and if I ever hurt your feelings again, I hope you will come right to me and let me know it at once, and I will try and explain it, or correct it. I trust you will forgive me, and I shall try and see you at the meeting Friday night and explain myself to you.

Your brother,

D. L. Moody [20]

∞

–Examining Our Own Hearts–

We've seen in this chapter just how essential humility is—not only in the life of a Christian, but also the life of a leader. We've seen that the greatest leader who ever walked this earth—God in human flesh—was also the greatest example of humility, taking on human flesh and, like a servant, washing dirty feet. Jesus even humbled Himself to the point of death. It's only when we come to the end of self that God can begin to use us. It's only when we set aside our own power that His power can work through us. And it's only when we stop taking the glory for ourselves that we can let the glory go to the One who really deserves it—God.

Having heard some of Moody's exhortations that we clothe ourselves with humility, it's time that we ask ourselves the same probing questions Moody posed at one of his leadership conferences:

∞

Have we been decreasing of late? Do we think less of ourselves and of our position than we did a year ago? Are we seeking to obtain some position of dignity; are we wanting to hold on to some title, and are we offended because we are not treated with the courtesy that we think is due us?[21]

∞

Take a moment to apply these questions to your own life. Can you see room for growth in your humility, your service? Do you consistently put self aside and others first?

Moody then went on to say,

∞

In one of his early epistles Paul calls himself the least of all the apostles. Later on he claims to be less than the least of all saints, and again, just before his death, humbly declares that he is the chief of sinners. Notice how he seems to have grown smaller and smaller in his own estimation. . . . And I do hope and pray that, as the days go by, we may each one of us feel like hiding ourselves, and let God have all the honor and glory.[22]

∞

Is God getting all the glory in your life? All the time?

MOODY
from the Pulpit

MY DEAR FRIENDS, I believe our only hope is to be filled with the Spirit of Christ. May God fill us, so that we shall be filled with meekness and humility. Let us take the hymn "O, to Be Nothing, Nothing," and make it the language of our hearts. It breathes the spirit of Him who said: "The Son can do nothing of Himself!"

> Oh, to be nothing, nothing!
> > Only to lie at His feet,
>
> A broken and emptied vessel,
> > For the Master's use made meek.
>
> Emptied, that He might fill me
> > As forth to His service I go;
>
> Broken, that so unhindered,
> > His life through me might flow.[23]

This One Thing I Do

When we look at all that Dwight Lyman Moody accomplished during more than forty years of ministry, we cannot help but wonder how he could possibly do so much. Biographers estimate he presented the gospel to millions of people through his evangelistic campaigns, quite a feat in the days before modern transportation helps and mass-media outlets that include radio and television. He started schools that trained large numbers of ministers and even more "gap men"—men and women who remained full-time workers or homemakers yet had the training to share the gospel with unbelievers and do productive works of service in their churches. The students and leaders who attended his schools and conferences came from all over the world—and carried his influence back with them to their native lands. His books were published by the hundreds of thousands and widely distributed.

All this from one solitary man who had no ministry training and was essentially illiterate when he started reaching out to the poor children in Chicago's worst district, the Sands.

One of Moody's mottoes was "Consecrate, then concentrate." Set yourself apart for God; then focus on the one supreme goal—that of glorifying God by bearing fruit for His kingdom. "Consecrate, then concentrate" were his words to the thousands who attended his conferences for leaders and ministry workers. Moody reminded his listeners that it's not our talents, our intellect, our abilities that God wants so much as our whole heart.

Yes, training is always good and desirable. It will enable us to do our service better, and we should strive toward that. But the best knowledge and skills are worthless if we don't have the right heart—a heart that, among other things, is . . .

- fully surrendered,

- abounding in love for people,

- passionate for the lost,

- constantly ready to pray,

- dependent upon the Spirit's power,

- dedicated to God's Word,

- trusting God,

- fervently committed to holiness, and

- marked by humility.

"This one thing I do" was another one of Moody's mottoes. In 1874, while in Scotland, Moody wrote to his friend Major Whittle, "I have done one thing on this trip, and the work is wonderful. *One thing* is my motto."[1]

As son William Moody wrote,

> Nothing could swerve him from this deep-rooted purpose of his life, and in all the various educational and publishing projects to which he gave his energy there was but one motive—the proclamation of the Gospel through multiplied agencies.[2]

Son-in-law Arthur Percy Fitt wrote,

> I do believe he had one supreme aim in life—to please God, more especially in the salvation of others through faith in Lord Jesus. All his plans in educational and other lines were tributary to that aim. All the elements of his character were conditioned by this devotion. He never lost his first love.[3]

A major theme of Moody's life is worth recalling: When we give our all to God, He can use us mightily. That doesn't mean He will use us in the same ways as He used Moody, or to achieve results similar to those He brought about through Moody's ministry. God gives every leader a different calling and a different stewardship; He places His workers strategically where He needs them most. It's not the size of our ministry or our results that count, but our willingness to take whatever God has entrusted to us and give ourselves wholly to that work. That's what it takes to allow Him to use us mightily.

Read slowly through Moody's powerful exhortations to "do one thing." Take some time now to ponder carefully what your life and ministry might look like—or *could* look like—if these exhortations from Moody drove your life.

∞

First give yourself up fully, wholly, and unreservedly to the Lord, and then put your life into some channel where you can be used. Consecrate, then concentrate. It is a good thing to get something definite, and go right about it. Make up your mind that your life is going to be given to that one thing. [4]

Let us be zealous of good works, let us go forth fired with the fires of heaven; let us make up our minds, that our money, our strength, our time, our all shall be given to Christ. We have but a little time to preach, to toil, to work.[5]

Let us be out and out for Christ; let us give no uncertain sound.[6]

The trouble with a great many men is that they spread themselves out over too much ground. They fail in everything. If they would only put their life into one channel, and keep it in, they would accomplish something. They make no impression, because they do a little work here and a little work there. . . . Lay yourselves on the altar of God, and then concentrate on some one work.[7]

And at the end of his life, Moody said to his ministry friends,

The honor of this world doesn't last; it is transient; it is passing away, and I don't believe any man or woman is fit for God's service that is looking for worldly preferment, worldly honors, worldly fame. Let us get it under our feet, let us rise above it, and seek the honor that comes down from above.[8]

Have you consecrated yourself?

Are you concentrating on one ultimate goal?

Can you say, "This one thing I do"?

Your answers will be shaped, of course, by whether you're in full-time ministry or you're a "gap man," as Moody would say—that is, ministry is not your occupation, but it's still an active part of your life. But no matter what your circumstances, your background, or your place in life, God *can* use you mightily . . . when you give yourself to Him mightily.

Consecrate, then concentrate.

And God will use you.

CHAPTER 1—A LIFE FULLY SURRENDERED TO GOD

1. As cited in J. Wilbur Chapman, *The Life and Work of D. L. Moody* (Philadelphia: American Bible House, 1900), 76.

2. W. H. Daniels, *D. L. Moody and His Work* (Hartford, Conn.: American Publishing, 1876), 28.

3. Ibid., 29.

4. William R. Moody, *The Life of D. L. Moody by His Son* (Chicago: Revell, 1900), 48.

5. *Northfield Echoes: Northfield Conference Addresses for 1898*, vol. 5, ed. Delavan L. Pierson (East Northfield, Mass.: Northfield Echoes, 1898), 14.

6. Ibid.

7. *Northfield Echoes: A Report of the Northfield Conferences for 1896*, vol. 3, ed. William Revell Moody and Delavan Leonard Pierson (East Northfield, Mass.: Rastall, 1896), 332.

8. William R. Moody, *Life of D. L. Moody*, 134.

9. Ibid.

10. *Northfield Echoes*, vol. 5, ed. Pierson, 3.

11. *Northfield Echoes: A Report of the Northfield Conferences for 1895*, vol. 2, ed. D. L. Pierson (East Northfield, Mass.: Rastall & McKinley, 1895), 173.

12. D. L. Moody, *The Gospel Awakening* (Hartford, Conn.: Betts & Co., 1878), 704.

13. *Northfield Echoes*, vol. 5, ed. Pierson, 4.

14. *Northfield Echoes*, vol. 3, ed. Moody and Pierson, 335.

15. D. L. Moody, *To All People: Glad Tidings Comprising Sermons, Bible Readings, Temperance Addresses, and Prayer-Meeting Talks* (New York: Treat, 1877), 14–15.

16. Ibid., 459.

17. Ibid., 14.

18. D. L. Moody, *The Overcoming Life* (Chicago: Moody, 1994), 115–16.

19. D. L. Moody, *New Sermons, Addresses, and Prayers by Dwight Lyman Moody* (St. John, New Brunswick, Canada.: Jones, 1878), 292.

20. William R. Moody, *Life of D. L. Moody,* 87.

21. Ibid., 97.

22. D. L. Moody, *The Home Work of D. L. Moody* (Chicago: Revell, 1886), 119.

23. John McDowell, *Dwight L. Moody* (Chicago: Revell, 1915), 22–23.

24. *Northfield Echoes*, vol. 3, ed. Moody and Pierson, 337.

25. *Northfield Echoes*, vol. 2, ed. Pierson, 337.

26. D. L. Moody, *Home Work of D. L. Moody,* 93.

27. D. L. Moody, *Moody's Stories: Incidents and Illustrations* (Chicago: Moody, 1899), 97–98.

28. D. L. Moody, *Home Work of D. L. Moody,* 93.

29. William R. Moody, *Life of D. L. Moody,* 87.

30. Letter from archives of the Crowell Library, ca. 1900, Moody Bible Institute, drawer 23.

31. As quoted in *Association Men*, 40, no. 5, February 1915, 245.

32. As quoted in John McDowell, *What D. L. Moody Means to Me* (East Northfield, Mass.: Northfield Schools, 1937), 30.

33. D. L. Moody, *New Sermons, Addresses, and Prayers*, 292.

CHAPTER 2—AN ABOUNDING LOVE FOR PEOPLE

1. William R. Moody, *The Life of D. L. Moody by His Son* (Chicago: Revell, 1900), 98.

2. "Moody Thirty Years Ago," newspaper clipping that cites an 1867 issue of *The Advance*, from archives of the Crowell Library, Moody Bible Institute, 269.2.

3. *D. L. Moody: A Man Who Never Asked Money for Himself* (Chicago: Moody Bible Institute, 1929), 5.

4. D. L. Moody, *Great Joy* (New York: Treat, 1877), 38–39.

5. Henry Drummond, "The Greatest Human I Ever Knew," in J. Wilbur Chapman, *The Life and Work of D. L. Moody* (Philadelphia: American Bible House, 1900), xiii.

6. As quoted in William R. Moody, *Life of D. L. Moody*, 219.

7. John McDowell, *Dwight L. Moody* (Chicago: Revell, 1915), 53.

8. Charles F. Goss, *Echoes from the Pulpit and Platform* (Hartford, Conn.: Worthington & Co., n.d.), 85.

9. Gamaliel Bradford, *D. L. Moody, A Worker in Souls* (New York: Doran, 1927), 108–109.

10. D. L. Moody, *Great Joy*, 38.

11. D. L. Moody, *The Gospel Awakening* (Hartford, Conn.: Betts & Co., 1878), 378–79.

12. Ibid., 379.

13. John Blanchard, *More Gathered Gold* (London: Evangelical Press, 1984), 193.

14. D. L. Moody, *Great Joy*, 36.

15. D. L. Moody, *To All People: Glad Tidings Comprising Sermons, Bible Readings, Temperance Addresses, and Prayer-Meeting Talks* (New York: Treat, 1877), 62.

16. *Northfield Echoes: A Report of the Northfield Conferences for 1895*, vol. 2, ed. D. L. Pierson (East Northfield, Mass.: Rastall & McKinley, 1895), 177.

17. D. L. Moody, *New Sermons, Addresses, and Prayers by Dwight Lyman Moody* (St. John, New Brunswick, Canada: Jones, 1878), 44.

18. William R. Moody, *Life of D. L. Moody*, 523.

19. *Northfield Echoes*, vol. 2, ed. Pierson, 177.

20. *Northfield Echoes: A Report of the Northfield Conferences for 1897*, vol. 4, ed. Delavan L. Pierson (East Northfield, Mass.: Northfield Echoes, 1897), 319.

21. D. L. Moody, *To the Work! To the Work!* (Chicago: Revell, 1884), 24.

22. Bradford, *D. L. Moody, A Worker in Souls*, 214.

23. R. A. Torrey, "D. L. Moody: Lessons from His Life and Death," *Australian Christian World*, 22 August 1902, 6.

24. As quoted in Emma Moody Powell, *Heavenly Destiny* (Chicago: Moody, 1943), 107.

25. *The Christian Workers Magazine*, February 1915, 355.

26. Lyle Dorsett, *A Passion for Souls* (Chicago: Moody, 1997), 301–302.

27. Ibid., 315.

28. Bradford, *D. L. Moody, A Worker in Souls*, 192.

29. A. P. Fitt, "D. L. Moody as a Letter Writer," *The Christian Workers Magazine*, December 1910, 272.

30. Letter dated April 25, 1887 from archives of the Crowell Library, Moody Bible Institute.

31. A. P. Fitt, *The Life of D. L. Moody* (Chicago: Moody, n.d.), 113–14.

32. Moody, *Great Joy*, 34.

33. Ibid., 36.

34. Moody, *To the Work!*, 28.

35. D. L. Moody, *Notes from My Bible* (Chicago: Revell, 1895), 166.

36. Moody, *To All People*, 56.

CHAPTER 3—A PASSION FOR REACHING LOST SOULS

1. D. L. Moody, *Moody's Stories: Incidents and Illustrations* (Chicago: Moody, 1899), 11.

2. Ibid.

3. William R. Moody, *The Life of D. L. Moody by His Son* (Chicago: Revell, 1900), 488.

4. Ibid., 295.

5. Ibid., 488.

6. D. L. Moody, *The Gospel Awakening* (Hartford, Conn.: Betts & Co., 1878), 154.

7. D. L. Moody, *The Home Work of D. L. Moody* (Chicago: Revell, 1886), 42.

8. As quoted in William R. Moody, *Life of D. L. Moody,* 204.

9. As quoted in T. J. Shanks, *D. L. Moody at Home* (Chicago: Revell, 1886), 41.

10. D. L. Moody, *Home Work of D. L. Moody,* 94.

11. Ibid., 71.

12. D. L. Moody, *The Faith Which Overcomes and Other Addresses* (London: Morgan & Scott, n.d.), 60.

13. D. L. Moody, *To All People: Glad Tidings Comprising Sermons, Bible Readings, Temperance Addresses, and Prayer-Meeting Talks* (New York: Treat, 1877), 339.

14. D. L. Moody, *The Faith Which Overcomes,* 58.

15. Ibid.

16. William R. Moody, *Life of D. L. Moody,* 183.

17. Ibid., 212.

18. Ibid., 184.

19. Ibid., 264.

20. Ibid., 497.

21. Ibid., 512.

22. Ibid., 283.

23. Letter from a woman who saw Moody in the winter of 1871–72, from archives of the Crowell Library, Moody Bible Institute, drawer ACC131C.

24. Quoting Rufus Clark in Gamaliel Bradford, *D. L. Moody, A Worker in Souls* (New York: Doran, 1927), 133.

25. J. McKinnon, *Recollections of D. L. Moody* (privately published, 1905), 19.

26. William R. Moody, *Life of D. L. Moody*, 295.

27. D. L. Moody, *The Gospel Awakening,* 209–210.

28. D. L. Moody, *The Overcoming Life* (Chicago: Moody, 1994), 58.

29. D. L. Moody, *The Faith Which Overcomes*, 63.

30. D. L. Moody, *To All People*, 51.

31. Joseph B. Banker, "Reminiscences of D. L. Moody," *The Institute Tie*, February 1903, 195.

32. D. L. Moody, *Grace, Prayer, and Work* (London: Morgan & Scott, n.d.), 355.

CHAPTER 4—A CONSTANT READINESS TO PRAY

1. William R. Moody, *The Life of D. L. Moody by His Son* (Chicago: Revell, 1900), 261.

2. R. A. Torrey, "D. L. Moody: Lessons from His Life and Death," *Australian Christian World*, 22 August 1902, 8.

3. *Northfield Echoes: Northfield Conference Addresses for 1900*, vol. 7, ed. Delavan L. Pierson (East Northfield, Mass.: Northfield Bookstore, 1900), 10.

4. William R. Moody, *Life of D. L. Moody*, 441.

5. Ibid., 508.

6. James M. Gray, *D. L. Moody: An Example and Inspiration of Christian Growth* (Chicago: Moody Bible Institute, n.d., but 1911 appears in an advertisement in this small pamphlet); archival collection of the Crowell Library, Moody Bible Institute, P269.2092 M817gr.

7. John McDowell, *What D. L. Moody Means to Me* (East Northfield, Mass.: Northfield Schools, 1937), 16–17.

8. Gamaliel Bradford, *D. L. Moody, A Worker in Souls* (New York: Doran, 1927), 107.

9. D. L. Moody, *The Gospel Awakening* (Hartford, Conn.: Betts & Co., 1878), 718.

10. Ibid., 753–54.

11. D. L. Moody, *To All People: Glad Tidings Comprising Sermons, Bible Readings, Temperance Addresses, and Prayer-Meeting Talks* (New York: Treat, 1877), 453.

12. D. L. Moody, *The Gospel Awakening*, 709.

13. Richard S. Rhodes, *Dwight Lyman Moody's Life Work and Latest Sermons* (Chicago: Jackson, 1900), 488–89.

14. Fred L. Norton, ed., *A College of Colleges*, session of 1889, (Chicago: Revell, 1889), 114.

15. Rhodes, *Dwight Lyman Moody's Life*, 488–89.

16. D. L. Moody, *The Gospel Awakening*, 607.

17. D. L. Moody, *To All People*, 477.

18. Rhodes, *Dwight Lyman Moody's Life*, 479.

19. *Northfield Echoes: A Report of the Northfield Conferences for 1897*, vol. 6, ed. Delavan L. Pierson (East Northfield, Mass.: Northfield Echoes, 1897), 356.

20. Rhodes, *Dwight Lyman Moody's Life*, 475–76.

21. Rhodes, *Dwight Lyman Moody's Life,* 484–85.

22. McDowell, *What D. L. Moody Means to Me*, 41.

23. Emma Moody Powell, *Heavenly Destiny* (Chicago: Moody, 1943), 171.

24. *Northfield Echoes: Northfield Conference Addresses for 1898*, vol. 5, ed. Delavan L. Pierson (East Northfield, Mass.: Northfield Echoes, 1898), 259.

CHAPTER 5—A DEPENDENCE UPON THE SPIRIT'S POWER

1. R. A. Torrey, "D. L. Moody: Lessons from His Life and Death," *Australian Christian World,* 22 August 1902, 10.

2. *Northfield Echoes: Northfield Conference Addresses for 1900*, vol. 7, ed. Delavan L. Pierson (East Northfield, Mass.: Northfield Bookstore, 1900) 8.

3. *The Institute Tie*, March 1901, 210–11.

4. Stanley N. Gundry, *Love Them In: The Life and Theology of D. L. Moody* (Chicago: Moody, 1999), 157.

5. D. L. Moody, *Secret Power* (Chicago: Revell, 1881), 34.

6. D. L. Moody, *Short Talks* (Chicago: Moody, 1900), 18–19.

7. D. L. Moody, *The Home Work of D. L. Moody* (Chicago: Revell, 1886), 97.

8. William R. Moody, *The Life of D. L. Moody by His Son* (Chicago: Revell, 1900), 149.

9. *The Institute Tie*, September 1900, 2.

10. D. L. Moody, *Secret Power*, 67.

11. *Northfield Echoes: Northfield Conference Addresses for 1898*, vol. 5, ed. Delavan L. Pierson (East Northfield, Mass.: Northfield Echoes, 1898), 258.

12. Ibid., 270.

13. D. L. Moody, *Secret Power*, preface.

14. D. L. Moody, *The Home Work of D. L. Moody*, 99.

15. D. L. Moody, *Secret Power*, 35–36.

16. Ibid., 13.

17. Ibid., 31–32.

18. Ibid., 43.

19. D. L. Moody, *The Gospel Awakening* (Hartford, Conn.: Betts & Co., 1878), 707.

20. D. L. Moody, *Secret Power*, 45–46.

21. Ibid., 46.

22. D. L. Moody, *To All People: Glad Tidings Comprising Sermons, Bible Readings, Temperance Addresses, and Prayer-Meeting Talks* (New York: Treat, 1877), 21.

23. D. L. Moody, *Moody's Stories: Incidents and Illustrations* (Chicago: Moody, 1899), 75–76.

CHAPTER 6—A DEDICATION TO GOD'S WORD

1. D. L. Moody, *Great Joy* (New York: Treat, 1877), 245.

2. Lyle Dorsett, *A Passion for Souls* (Chicago: Moody, 1997), 393.

3. Citing Charles R. Erdman in Wilbur M. Smith, *An Annotated Bibliography of D. L. Moody* (Chicago: Moody, 1948), 125.

4. William R. Moody, *The Life of D. L. Moody by His Son* (Chicago: Revell, 1900), 441.

5. Ibid., 114.

6. Ibid., 492.

7. D. L. Moody, *Great Joy*, 234.

8. William R. Moody, *Life of D. L. Moody*, 491–92.

9. Ibid., 492.

10. D. L. Moody, *Moody's Stories: Incidents and Illustrations* (Chicago: Moody, 1899), 84–85.

11. D. L. Moody, *The Home Work of D. L. Moody* (Chicago: Revell, 1886), 106–107.

12. D. L. Moody, *Great Joy*, 236–37.

13. William R. Moody, *Life of D. L. Moody*, 258.

14. Ibid., 278.

15. Newspaper clipping titled "Moody Talks of Rest," from archives of the Crowell Library, Moody Bible Institute, 269.2.

16. D. L. Moody, *Men of the Bible* (Chicago: Moody, 1898), 32.

17. *Northfield Echoes: Northfield Conference Addresses for 1900*, vol. 7, ed. Delavan L. Pierson (East Northfield, Mass.: Northfield Bookstore, 1900), 8–9.

18. Ibid., 9.

19. D. L. Moody, *Moody's Stories*, 22.

20. *Northfield Echoes*, vol. 7, ed. Pierson, 19.

21. William R. Moody, *Life of D. L. Moody*, 492.

22. T. J. Shanks, *D. L. Moody at Home* (Chicago: Revell, 1886), 264.

23. Quoting Charles R. Erdman, Smith, *Annotated Bibliography*, 124–25.

24. Letter dated September 10, 1895, from archives of the Crowell Library, Moody Bible Institute.

Chapter 7—A Faith That Believes and Trusts God

1. Lyle Dorsett, *A Passion for Souls* (Chicago: Moody, 1997), 279.

2. D. L. Moody, *To All People: Glad Tidings Comprising Sermons, Bible Readings, Temperance Addresses, and Prayer-Meeting Talks* (New York: Treat, 1877), 170.

3. Ibid., 174.

4. Ibid., 446–47.

5. Ibid., 176.

6. Ibid., 174–75.

7. *Northfield Echoes: A Report of the Northfield Conferences for 1897*, vol. 4, ed. Delavan L. Pierson (East Northfield, Mass.: Northfield Echoes, 1897), 353.

8. D. L. Moody, *The Gospel Awakening* (Hartford, Conn.: Betts & Co., 1878), 708.

9. Ibid., 459.

10. D. L. Moody, *The Overcoming Life* (Chicago: Moody, 1994), 10.

11. Charles F. Goss, *Echoes from the Pulpit and Platform* (Hartford, Conn.: Worthington & Co., n.d.), 625–26.

12. *Northfield Echoes: Northfield Conference Addresses for 1900*, vol. 7, ed. Delavan L. Pierson (East Northfield, Mass.: Northfield Bookstore, 1900), 19.

13. D. L. Moody, *Wondrous Love and Other Gospel Addresses* (London: Pickering & Inglis, 1876), 22.

14. D. L. Moody, *To All People*, 17.

15. D. L. Moody, *Moody's Stories: Incidents and Illustrations* (Chicago: Moody, 1899), 28–29.

16. Ibid., 120.

17. D. L. Moody, *The Overcoming Life*, 122–23.

18. D. L. Moody, *New Sermons, Addresses, and Prayers by Dwight Lyman Moody* (St. John, New Brunswick, Canada: Jones, 1878), 25.

19. D. L. Moody, *To the Work! To the Work!* (Chicago: Revell, 1884), 46.

20. *Northfield Echoes: A Report of the Northfield Conferences for 1895*, vol. 2, ed. D. L. Pierson (East Northfield, Mass.: Rastall & McKinley, 1895), 175.

21. D. L. Moody, *Moody's Stories*, 15.

22. D. L. Moody, *New Sermons, Addresses, and Prayers*, 353.

CHAPTER 8—A FERVENT COMMITMENT TO HOLINESS

1. William R. Moody, *The Life of D. L. Moody by His Son* (Chicago: Revell, 1900), 368.

2. D. L. Moody, *The Overcoming Life* (Chicago: Moody, 1994), 58.

3. D. L. Moody, *Moody's Stories: Incidents and Illustrations* (Chicago: Moody, 1899), 77.

4. D. L. Moody, *The Faith Which Overcomes and Other Addresses* (London: Morgan & Scott, n.d.), 59.

5. *Northfield Echoes: A Report of the Northfield Conferences for 1897*, vol. 4, ed. Delavan L. Pierson (East Northfield, Mass.: Northfield Echoes, 1897), 320.

6. Ibid., 321–22.

7. D. L. Moody, *The Faith Which Overcomes*, 61–62.

8. D. L. Moody, *The Overcoming Life*, 58.

9. *Northfield Echoes: A Report of the Northfield Conferences for 1896,* vol. 3, ed. William Revell Moody and Delavan Leonard Pierson (East Northfield, Mass.: Rastall, 1896), 112.

10. D. L. Moody, *Great Joy* (New York: Treat, 1877), 498.

11. *Northfield Echoes: Northfield Conference Addresses for 1898*, vol. 5, ed. Delavan L. Pierson (East Northfield, Mass.: Northfield Echoes, 1898), 268–69.

12. D. L. Moody, *Short Talks* (Chicago: Moody, 1900), 57.

13. D. L. Moody, *Fifty Sermons and Evangelistic Talks* (Cleveland: Barton, 1899), 175–76.

14. D. L. Moody, *Short Talks*, 31.

15. D. L. Moody, *Moody's Stories*, 83.

16. D. L. Moody, *To All People: Glad Tidings, Comprising Sermons, Bible Readings, Temperance Addresses, and Prayer-Meeting Talks* (New York: Treat, 1877), 448.

17. D. L. Moody, *The Home Work of D. L. Moody* (Chicago: Revell, 1886), 111–12.

18. D. L. Moody, *The Faith Which Overcomes,* 7.

19. D. L. Moody, *To All People,* 392.

20. D. L. Moody, *The Faith Which Overcomes,* 36.

21. Ibid., 10.

22. *Northfield Echoes,* vol. 5, ed. Pierson, 249.

Chapter 9—A Heart Marked by Humility

1. "Reminiscences of Dwight L. Moody," *The Christian Workers Magazine*, February 1915, 352–53. This particular reminiscence is from A. F. Gaylord.

2. William R. Moody, *The Life of D. L. Moody by His Son* (Chicago: Revell, 1900), 584.

3. *Northfield Echoes: Northfield Conference Addresses for 1900*, vol. 7, ed. Delavan L. Pierson (East Northfield, Mass.: Northfield Bookstore, 1900), 12.

4. William R. Moody, *Life of D. L. Moody*, 148.

5. D. L. Moody, *The Overcoming Life* (Chicago: Moody, 1994), 83–84.

6. *Northfield Echoes: A Report of the Northfield Conferences for 1896*, vol. 3, ed. William Revell Moody and Delavan Leonard Pierson (East Northfield, Mass.: Rastall, 1896), 386.

7. D. L. Moody, *The Overcoming Life*, 82.

8. *Northfield Echoes: Northfield Conference Addresses for 1898*, vol. 5, ed. Delavan L. Pierson (East Northfield, Mass.: Northfield Echoes, 1898), 250.

9. *Northfield Echoes*, vol. 3, ed. Moody and Pierson, 332.

10. D. L. Moody, *Short Talks* (Chicago: Moody, 1900), 21.

11. D. L. Moody, *The Gospel Awakening* (Hartford, Conn.: Betts & Co., 1878), 706.

12. D. L. Moody, *To All People: Glad Tidings Comprising Sermons, Bible Readings, Temperance Addresses, and Prayer-Meeting Talks* (New York: Treat, 1877), 440–41.

13. Ibid., 390–91.

14. Ibid., 391.

15. *Northfield Echoes*, vol. 5, ed. Pierson, 250.

16. *Northfield Echoes*, vol. 3, ed. Moody and Pierson, 333.

17. Ibid., 386.

18. Ibid., 387.

19. William R. Moody, *Life of D. L. Moody*, 110–11.

20. Letter from archives of the Crowell Library, Moody Bible Institute, Historical Room, 242.4, T8910 (vol. 1, 1854–79).

21. *Northfield Echoes*, vol. 3, ed. Moody and Pierson, 389.

22. Ibid.

23. D. L. Moody, *The Overcoming Life*, 92.

Conclusion—This One Thing I Do

1. William R. Moody, *The Life of D. L. Moody by His Son* (Chicago: Revell, 1900), 502.

2. Ibid.

3. Quoting A. P. Fitt in *The Congregationalist and Christian World*, 12 November 1914, 624.

4. *Northfield Echoes: A Report of the Northfield Conferences for 1896*, vol. 3, ed. William Revell Moody and Delavan Leonard Pierson (East Northfield, Mass.: Rastall, 1896), 113.

5. *Northfield Echoes: A Report of the Northfield Conferences for 1895*, vol. 2, ed. D. L. Pierson (East Northfield, Mass.: Rastall & McKinley, 1895), 46.

6. D. L. Moody, *The Overcoming Life* (Chicago: Moody, 1994), 52.

7. George Sweeting, "D. L. Moody: His Steps to Excellence," *Moody Monthly*, February 1985, 32.

8. *Northfield Echoes: Northfield Conference Addresses for 1900*, vol. 7, ed. Delavan L. Pierson (East Northfield, Mass.: Northfield Bookstore, 1900), 19–20.

If after reading this book you find you would like to read more about Dwight L. Moody and his life and ministry, you'll want to read two excellent biographies—one that's presently out of print, and one that's contemporary to our day.

Before D. L. Moody died, he knew that upon his death many writers and publishers would be eager to capitalize on his popularity and quickly flood the book market with biographies. He was concerned that these rushed productions would be carelessly written and might contain inaccuracies. With that in mind, he authorized his son William to write his official life story after he died. William's fine and thorough work was published in 1900 by the Fleming H. Revell Company and is titled *The Life of D. L. Moody by His Son*. The book was widely published then and again in 1930, when it was updated, so copies are not hard to find on used book Web sites such as www.abebooks.com or www.bookfinder.com.

My favorite modern-day biography is *A Passion for Souls: The Life of D. L. Moody,* by Lyle Dorsett, released in 1997 by Moody Publishers. Dorsett's excellent presentation is comprehensive yet highly readable, and warm yet balanced. The book is readily available through local Christian bookstores.

Since 1894, Moody Publishers has been dedicated to equip and motivate people to advance the cause of Christ by publishing evangelical Christian literature and other media for all ages, around the world. Because we are a ministry of the Moody Bible Institute of Chicago, a portion of the proceeds from the sale of this book go to train the next generation of Christian leaders.

If we may serve you in any way in your spiritual journey toward understanding Christ and the Christian life, please contact us at www.moodypublishers.com.

"All Scripture is God-breathed and is useful for teaching, rebuking, correcting and training in righteousness, so that the man of God may be thoroughly equipped for every good work."
—2 TIMOTHY 3:16, 17

MOODY
PUBLISHERS

THE NAME YOU CAN TRUST®

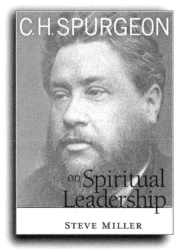

ISBN: 0-8024-1064-2

In the realm of spiritual leadership, more than any other, seeing biblical leadership in action is critical to becoming a better leader.

So, Bible teacher and church leader Steve Miller shows us a vibrant picture of one of the nineteenth century's stellar spiritual leaders, Charles Haddon Spurgeon, in this compilation of sermons, prayers and writings on leadership.

These basic disciplines and character traits not only made Spurgeon a great spiritual leader, they can make you one, too – if you'll take this enriching opportunity to read, reflect and be changed.

MOODY
PUBLISHERS

THE NAME YOU CAN TRUST.

1-800-678-6928   www.MoodyPublishers.com

D.L. MOODY ON SPIRITUAL LEADERSHIP TEAM

ACQUIRING EDITOR:
Mark Tobey

COPY EDITOR:
Jim Vincent

BACK COVER COPY:
Anne Perdicaris

COVER DESIGN:
Paetzold Associates

INTERIOR DESIGN:
Paetzold Associates

PRINTING AND BINDING:
Color House Graphics

The typeface for the text of this book is
Berkeley